EVERYDAY REVOLUTION

Finding clarity, conviction and joy with Feminism.

AMRITA PURKAYASTHA

ISBN 979-8-88641-562-9

Dedication

To the women with messy hair, kind heart and curious mind.

To the women who write their own stories — on paper or otherwise.

Contents

1. The One on My Privilege, Revolution and More... 7

1. *Childhood* **17**
The one about innocence, parenting and memories

2. Unwantedness 19
3. Lessons in *Maryada, Sharam & Bipod* 35
4. Growing Up in a Binary World of
   Mard and *Aurat* 53

2. *Marriage* **65**
The one about rituals, family and pleasure

5. Shadi – The Problem in the Recipe 67
6. The Ideal *Bahu* Template 89
7. "*Haq se Maango*":
   Sex, Intimacy and Compatibility 103

3. *Motherhood* **115**
The one about choice, ovaries and pedestalization

8. To Birth or Not to Birth 117
9. "*Maa Toh Maa Hoti Hai*" –
   The Pedestalization That Hurts 131

4. Beauty   **143**
The one on body image, shame and self-worth

10. Beauty = Love: The Power and Currency of
Being Pretty   145
11. Beauty Regimes, Billboards and the
Conundrum of Choice   161
12. Dear Body-Shamers – F*ck You!   175

5. Work   **187**
The one on corporations, capitalism and networking

13. What Work Means?   189
14. Corporate *Taam Jhaam* – A Game of Toxicity
and Money   203

6. The Last Word   **217**
15. On Re-Imaging the World
Through a Feminist Lens   219

References   *229*
Acknowledgement   *233*

1

The One on My Privilege, Revolution and More...

I am somewhat of a clichéd 90s kid, who grew up with an obsession for Cricket, Bollywood and getting an engineering degree. An over-thinking Indian, millennial woman in her 30s, who has always been curious about the workings of the world and a tad bit conflicted about her own life choices, I am a marketeer by the day, a culture and gender researcher by night and an obsessive meme-lover in between. I am a Bengali, born in Assam, brought up in Gujarat, influenced by Punjabi friends and Music, which means I use both *Thakurer Kripa* and *Mata Rani Ki Kripa* interchangeably.

I also use the word *yaar* way too often in conversations, which is something my Rabindranath-worshiping Bengali parents take as a personal attack. I have lived across Jaipur, Paris, Bhubaneswar, Delhi, Nanded, Dubai, Pondicherry and Mumbai, which means that I have haggled and negotiated with hundreds of *Bhaiyyas, Annas, Bhaus,* and more notably, with Uncle Patriarchy all through my life in different forms and sizes. IYKYK!

The story of my life started much before my own premature birth. It started in the late 1960s when my baba migrated to India from Bangladesh during the partition of East Pakistan amidst unimaginable chaos and violence. At the age of 14, with his father grievously injured and the rest of his family missing, Baba had to quickly grow up to survive. He spent his whole life living like people who felt lucky to be alive. My 'Ma,' one amongst 4 sisters, was brought up by a matriarch, who somehow mustered the courage to educate them at a time and place where higher education for girls was revolutionary.

Unbeknown to me, throughout my extended childhood as the younger sibling, my parents struggled with migration, isolation, crushing financial troubles and more. They must have learnt across many years of experiencing dislocation and violence that realism and practicality are not just necessary but inevitable in this world. Yet, somehow, despite all of that, they still believed in wonder, curiosity and revolution a tad bit more.

Fuelled by my parents' incorrigible optimism, despite some rather grim situations, I grew up thinking I was special and made for big things. My parents' hyper-busy middle-class lives made them decent caregivers and I had what psychologists might say a 'well-adjusted' childhood. All my life, I have had food to eat, clothes to flaunt and access to great books and crappy movies. I grew up feeling entitled to a life full of opportunities and possibilities.

As I touched 30, I became an elder to many, even aunty to some, and that awkward, uncomfortable feeling of being an adult also brought along something precious – hindsight. A clearer, more rational evaluation of my life, came along with pre-mature greying, wrinkles and cellulite. I accepted, rather grudgingly, that I wasn't going to win an Oscar or a Nobel and definitely not both. The speech I had been secretly practising in the shower all my life was probably never going to be televised. I probably wasn't the chosen one and even my birthmarks didn't have some glorious past life significance. Through quiet introspection, I also realized I wasn't special or particularly gifted. And with such dull pragmatism came a core-jerking realization – I was still *god-damned* blessed to get this life to live.

All my life, I had been blissfully blind to the elite categories of privileges I enjoyed. I was not just a woman – I was upper-caste, cis-gendered, heterosexual. My mediocre life, devoid of exemplary talent or enviable luxuries, was still statistically a unicorn. I started to interrogate the extent of my privilege, the consequences of those and became aware that people who are different from me experience the world in ways I might never fully know about.

And despite that, I must try. I came to realize that when we become conscious of our privilege, we feel compelled to use it in some way – building a stage for others and not necessarily giving a glorious speech ourselves. Because that's the thing about privilege – everybody has something that somebody else doesn't. But being conscious of the specific ways in which we have been lucky in this world throws the spotlight right in the face of our misplaced sense of entitlement in this completely random, inexplicable world.

The principles of equality and justice became desperately important, as I started seeing how unfair the accident of birth was, even if I had personally benefitted from it in many ways. With many belittling personal failures came much-needed humility. With a prolonged struggle with anxiety and shaky mental health came some understanding of the human mind. With the death of loved ones and living through a full year in an apocalyptic, soul-crushing COVID world came a renewed appreciation for life.

Much before the onset of wrinkles and wisdom in my 30s, I knew I was a feminist. Even before I came across the word, I realized what it meant to be a woman and that it was a massive disadvantage in this world. Before Beyoncé sang about it or Dior made it into a cool T-shirt art. But it was still too late to protect myself from internalizing patriarchy to my bone. All the access I have had to great books and crappy movies still showed me a world from a man's perspective. The world I grew up in was run, fought and imagined by men. I didn't learn about women's ambitions, sexuality, points of view until much later. I learnt about feminine desirability and beauty as explained by men. I learnt about a model of success and ambition that was defined by men. I grew up in a world where love was imagined as sacrificial, mostly in relation to other men in my life. I lived in a world where my personhood 'as a woman' was diluted in many ways without me ever fully understanding it.

It was a world where I was shamed into limiting the space I was taking with my body and thoughts. I felt an inexplicable sting in my heart when I was catcalled, spoken over and under-estimated. I felt rudely shaken out of my assumption of safety and respect. In those moments of epiphany and heartbreak, something changed forever.

As I came across Feminism – the ideology, the history, the books – I also came to know fellow feminists, authors, creators and revolutionaries. Feminist writers made me understand myself better; they made me understand the world better. Through them, I found a way to be hopeful even when I was heartbroken. I found conviction, even when I was fearful. It felt radical for a chronic people-pleaser like me to embrace Feminism. As I found the courage to call out problematic behaviours or started prioritizing myself over appropriateness, I also worried about being left all alone. But I found new friends, new thoughts, new language. I found clarity, conviction and community.

Armed with feminist thoughts, as I started unravelling how I had internalized the patriarchal gender construct all my life, I felt a desperate need to know other women's stories. Inspired by the Blue Stockings Club of the late 1900s, I started a research project titled – **100 Women Project.** On this journey, I met experts and activists, a cousin's friends, and my friend's colleagues. From the activist in rural Karnataka to the corporate boss in Bombay, from the gynaecologist in Romania to the sassy, blue-haired copywriter in Bangalore. Not all women claimed to be Feminists. In fact, most didn't. I didn't try to change their minds. I knew Feminism has had a bad reputation and it is one of the sly ways patriarchy fights back and invalidates this movement. But in my journey, the tags didn't matter when women opened up about their lives. At the heart of our life experiences was an undeniable mirror that reflected a common experience of living in a gender-inequal world. And *that* tag was always undeniable.

In my research, I had a simple template to look at major themes of women's lives through the lens of gender. We discussed some of our most formative experiences through our **Childhood** years, we discussed our **Marriage**, our **Motherhood** journey, our approach to **Beauty** and our experience at **Work**. Sometimes, we contrasted our experiences with those of the men in our lives, and sometimes, we dwelled deeper into our own instincts and choices. The conversations would often swing from personal to political. They would turn from discussing equal pay to period cramps, bikini wax to barbie dolls, breastfeeding to Bollywood songs, and many a time, ended up being hours of philosophical discussion about life and Thai curry recipes. I shared my experiences as much as they shared theirs. I could look into their eyes, see their nervous laughter, hold their hands and know their stories. These discussions gave us the opportunity to evaluate our lives together. A chance to relive, love and caress a life lived.

Some experiences were insightful, others infuriating. Some were brave and others were heart-breaking. Most stories didn't have heroic cliff-hanging endings, although many of them did. Most were simply ordinary women, sharing anecdotes of fighting biases and sexism in their families, streets, offices and more importantly, inside their own heads.

As I went beyond my echo chamber, connected with women with different life experiences and world views, I also spent a good deal of time going back over my own life. In my 30s, it felt a bit late to really know myself for the first time. I realized that even after years of prohibitively expensive education, I didn't quite have an understanding of this world and how my personal choices were shaped by it. It is through the experiences of other women that I found a way to make sense of my own.

Their stories became a window to the world and its functioning. They gave me an insight into how things worked and the required courage to fight it.

I also dived into psychology and neuroscience, economics and culture studies to start connecting the dots and see repeated patterns in the world. And slowly, as I found sisterhood and solidarity with these incredible women, I also found patterns and interconnectedness in the research and studies.

The interplay between omnipresent patriarchy and the human mind's craving for cognitive closure or learned stimulus. The connection between the consumerist economy and the undefined problem of self-worth amongst housewives. The interconnectedness of our imperialist history and unachievable beauty ideals. The overlapping structures were as interesting to unravel as the brave stories I heard.

Across the stories of my life and the ones I heard from other women, there was something undeniably common – the fact that our experiences are covered in societal, cultural and emotional dust and that they are often tangled by shame, guilt and fears. We are run by stories that play out in our heads and we don't know what kinds of assumptions rule us until we pause and reflect. This book then came to life as an attempt to re-evaluate our lives with curiosity and courage and to cast a harsh glare at the realities that we have come to know as universal and inevitable. What we allow continues and, in many ways, most of us have allowed ourselves to be harmed, hurt and changed by this world.

For the readers, to unravel your true self, brush off some of the metaphorical dust from your memories and find some semblance of closure and comfort, you will find simple writing prompts at the end of each chapter. Through many years of struggling to reconcile with my emotions myself, I have learnt that writing could be a tremendous aide for our psychological digging.

In this noisy world, it is incredibly therapeutic to be listened to, and writing, more than anything, is a way to get heard unconditionally. The statistics and stories in these chapters may leave you breathless, moved, laughing, devastated or anything else on the emotional spectrum, but most of all, I hope it leaves you inspired to write. Use these blank pages to look at your experiences and the world with a fresh perspective. At the end of each chapter, I urge you to reflect on your own life – think of the ways gender had impacted your experience of that part of your life. Through the blank pages, talk to your own self, past, present and future.

If women can re-craft our inner worlds and re-imagine the world out there through that, we can change it for the better. It is through our everyday lives lived with clarity, conviction and joy can we create a revolution. Armed with research and stories of our own and women around us, we can, in our own ways, help build a better human experience. We can find a way to unlearn and re-learn some of our **childhood** lessons, we can redefine the pivotal institution of **marriage**, we can recraft the experience of **parenting**, we could create a world of **beauty** without shame and redefine what fulfilling **work** can look like in this world. It is with this rather filmy and absurdly idealistic goal that I ventured into writing this book many years back.

During one of his theatrical *gyaan* sessions, many years back, my baba taught me a beautiful Bengali line, "*Lodai Lodai Lodai Chai, Lodai kore Bachte Chai.*"

It roughly translates as "let us fight and hustle always, as long as we live."

To never accept the status quo is the only human way to live on this planet. To try and make our world a better, fairer place in whichever foolish, insignificant way we can is the only worthwhile way to spend our limited time. It is abundantly clear to me that everything that had to be said about equality or fairness or justice has probably already been said by many in many ways throughout our history. But it seems like many weren't listening. And hence, it must be said again. And yet again. Even if it is by an average, meme-loving, middle-aged woman who makes PPTs for a living.

Childhood

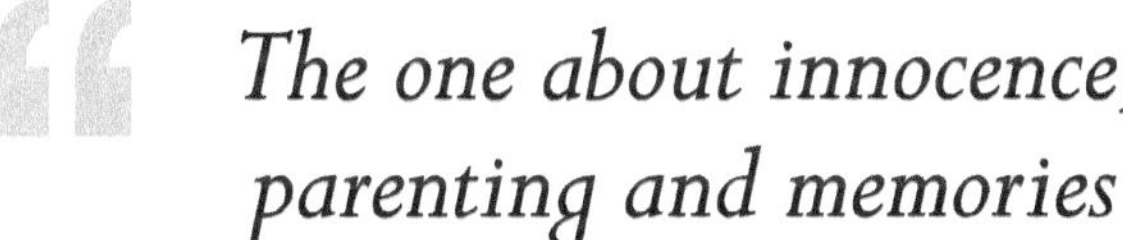

2

Unwantedness

The one about the misplaced guilt of being born a girl

"My Thamma (grandmom) had told my pregnant mom, "Meye hole, Kashi," roughly translating as "Send me to die if it is a girl." I heard of this story when I was 6 years old and remember feeling deeply ashamed and guilty. I felt responsible for disappointing my Thamma and cried for days. I started hating all the girly things I liked otherwise; I wanted short hair, drew a moustache on my face and begged my mother to somehow make me a boy."

"I had read in civics that child marriage was illegal and infanticide was a crime. And yet, I heard stories around my community and neighbourhood of girls aged 12 or 14 years old who were married off. Or the 3rd daughter being left behind in the hospital and never brought home. My parents' reaction to such stories was that of nonchalance. I learnt that "aisa toh hota hi hai" and that the rules of justice and fairness didn't apply to us girls."

"When I was 5 years old and my elder sister was 8, my mom was pregnant. I remember poojas and jagratas that *were arranged so that we could get a brother. I heard so many relatives and neighbours give my mother nuskhas to have a boy. It was clear to me that boys mattered more."*

"My younger cousin brother always used to get a larger portion of halwa and a larger share of dry fruits from my dadi. These were not food; these were symbols of love. We sisters knew he was loved much more than us."

I don't remember understanding the meaning of gender or what it meant to be a girl till I was about 10 or 11 years old. Our small migrant home with the four of us, thousands of miles away from our extended family, was an egalitarian world. My sister and I always got the *exact* same number of prawns, matched in shape and weight, whenever *chingri curry* was made at home. Our parents seemed too busy making a living to worry about who would light their pyre in absence of a *ghar ka chirag*. A short story from the Hindi syllabus in our CBSE curriculum is possibly my earliest memory of witnessing patriarchy. It was one of those long-drawn texts, which was supposed to teach us something completely forgettable, like alliteration or synonyms or correct use of pronouns. But this story ended up teaching me something entirely different.

In the story, the author was visiting the home of a friend and observed something rather strange. The little girl of the host was fed last during dinner, given leftovers and was generally given no affection or attention. Their son, in contrast, was encouraged to recite a poem, pampered, cuddled and excessively fed. Towards the end of his visit, the author quietly finds a moment alone with the girl. He gives her a toy and asks why she thought she was made to eat last or wasn't allowed to sit with the guests.

As she hesitantly accepted the toy, she replies succinctly, almost with a nonchalance – *"Ladki hoon na?"* (I am a girl; that's why!) This is the point where the story ended and that line was left with no explanation. We readers were left with just this sentence as food for thought, for deliberation and possibly, introspection.

The class discussion that followed was mostly on prose – sentence making, synonyms, etc. But I remember sitting silently with a deep sense of grief for the girl's quiet submission. My uninformed, protected worldview was shaken. As I grasped the full meaning of that climactic dialogue, it was heart-breaking to know the bitter truth for the first time. The truth that I later experienced in many ways. The simple truth that being born a girl in this World meant being a little *less*.

Our childhood years are the most foundational time of our lives. Most parts of our personalities, aptitude and abilities start building in these years. From Freud to Skinner to Piaget, most psychologists have formed direct, statistically valid connections between our adult personality and aptitude with our childhood experiences. As adults, we often don't know how our mind works or know the origin of many of our feelings and actions – why do we love something instinctively, or why do we hate *Bhindi* or love the colour yellow? How do some of us become good at believing in ourselves, and how do some of us become better at taking risks? Our development of language, comprehension and reasoning has no active awareness, but psychologists throughout history have linked these to our childhood environment and experiences.

In India, many girls who survive the 9 months inside their mother's bodies, experience the brutality of unwantedness in covert and overt ways once they are out. Research done in 2018 on thousands of households in Maharashtra found the phenomenon of *"Nakusal Nakoshi"* (literally translated as unwanted.) [1] This is a name given to the 2nd of 3rd girl child by her parents with a superstitious belief that naming her such would bless the family with a male child. A similar phenomenon is seen in Tamil Nadu, where such girls are named *"vedampunoo."*

It's not hard to imagine that hundreds of these girls named *Nakusas* or *Vedampunoo* spend their whole life in humiliation and shame. The proof that the value of a girl's life is less than that of a boy's in our society doesn't just stay in the files of Niti Ayog or the Women and Health Ministry. It reaches a little girl's tender world much before she can understand terms like discrimination and injustice.

This preference for the male child is systemic and not just an individual preference. Parents across cultures know that the quality of life of the child and, in many ways, their own lives would markedly be better if the child happens to be born with a penis. The world we live in is a marketplace. It is driven by economics, and it is a place where the worth of the male child is simply much more. A boy is an asset; a future breadwinner who brings in a wife, who, in turn, doubles up as an unpaid nurse for ageing parents. And when they die, Hindu tradition dictates their pyre is lit by their son, which would give the parents the much-advertised *mukti*.

A girl, on the other hand, is considered a liability – an expense which has little or no return. Her dowry would cost the family a fortune, and after marriage, she is considered part of her husband's family and may end up living away, making caregiving impractical. The preference for the male child is an expression which shows the fundamental disadvantage of being born a woman in this world.

We cannot fully understand the effect it has on girls when in their formative years, they experience a form of unwantedness. Sometimes, it is not overt; it is hearsay, an anecdote repeated by a relative or something we overhear the neighbours talk about. Some of us sense this when a neighbour sympathizes with our parents since we don't have a brother. Some of us feel this when our brother has the imported tennis bat, and we must use cloth napkins instead of sanitary pads. Some of us hear stories of how our Mausi or Bua is disowned by her husband as she gives birth to their third daughter. Some of us experience this via stories of little girls thrown away in hospitals, backyards or dustbins. We realize how the world could be much worse for us and we should be thankful to be alive in the first place.

Families tell their girls in million small and big ways that their aspirations, comfort or even safety is far less of a priority. It imprints in little girls that she is not entitled to humanity, let alone equality. Those acts of discrimination and visible inequity that we learn to ignore and live with, leave a profound imprint on our personalities, choices and instincts. This has a deep, long-lasting psychological impact. This feeling that the world wants you less imprints in you that you *are* less. This happens across types and forms of homes: urban, rural, educated, poor, middle-income, upper-caste, etc.

Most women experience their inequal place in the world, albeit in different ways and at different stages of their lives. The lucky few have the access to read it in books or see it in movies and are introduced to this concept theoretically. They might develop a way of addressing this intellectually. But many experience the unwantedness first-hand, during the formative growing-up years, which, in many ways, lead to an unquestioned acceptance of it as a way of life.

When inequality is so blatant, one starts to assume that as normal. When it is everywhere, one doesn't really see it as a problem. If it was in some place and not others, we could have possibly called that out. But we see our mothers, sisters and cousins treated a certain way and that just gets accepted as the norm. Add to that the flawed unquestioned notion of always respecting our elders, which is a fundamental tenet of Indian culture. These oppressive, hurtful behaviours start finding long-lasting legitimacy in our minds.

We internalize this even before we have the strength of heart or reason of the mind to resist. Many years later, we women can intellectually reason that this behaviour was unfair and faulty. But it takes deep introspection to recognize that somehow, these have seeped deep into our own instincts. After many decades, as grown women, we still don't question the inequality and the blatant difference in the way the world treats us and the men in our lives. Often, we don't even see it as a problem and meekly try and live with it, accepting patriarchy as universal truth.

Psychologists and behavioural scientists say that there is a vulnerability in the make-up of the human mind. Self-love is a trait learnt by imitation. Our brain doesn't develop self-love unless it sees someone else love us. We cannot value ourselves unless we are valued deeply by someone in our formative years. It is through someone's unbridled love and care that we learn to develop a positive self-image and thereby, develop an ability to care for ourselves and others. Being rejected, being unloved or living through a life that is less valued by the ones we love, leaves an imprint on our psyche that we are often unable to unpack in our grown adult lives. Even when we defy, there is fatigue. Even when we comply, there is inexplicable guilt.

The feeling of unwantedness and rejection could have different ramifications in our lives. Some of us defy, some comply but many never fully undo the scar and relive the pattern. Research says that women who were discriminated against as children are three to six times more likely to experience and endure intimate partner violence in their adult lives. In fact, the impact of childhood environment on adult relationships has been corroborated by multiple theories in psychology. How we approach attachment as adults depends, to a very large extent, on our childhood experiences. One of the most prominent studies on this subject is The Attachment Theory, pioneered by John Bowlby. It categorizes adult relationships into 3 types: secured, anxious and avoidant. It is backed by neuro-psychological studies that have found that by 8 months, babies start understanding what it means to be loved and how it should be demonstrated. With a healthy relationship with parents, where kids can go out and explore the world, and feel safe and protected, they are more likely to have secured attachment in adult relationships. Avoidant and anxious attachment styles in adult relations are often the result of some form of early childhood trauma – abandonment, indifference, etc. Most of us are largely unconscious of this awkward psychological inheritance from our caregivers.

Linking this to research on adolescent happiness and health possibly gives us a window into different approaches men and women have towards adult romantic relationships. The global research titled "Growing Up Unequal," based on more than 200,000 young people in 42 countries released in 2016, [2] concluded that girls were far more unhappy and reportedly unhealthy in their growing up years compared to boys. As a disproportionate number of girls spend their early childhood bound in rules, constraints, indifference and abuse, as grown women, they are far more likely to have an anxious approach to relationships. As the world shows little girls a little less encouragement, love and affection, she grows up yearning for validation and believes that as an adult, being loved will be her ultimate redemption. Simply put, as little girls grow up in an inequal world, they grow up to be women who expect their relationship to define them, rescue them or complete them. That leads to women having far more anxious and avoidant relationships compared to men.

But the good news is that the human mind has the ability to heal almost everything. It is not just the experiences that define us. It is reflecting on them that does. It is the lesson we learn from them that does. The right meme and the right therapist could help us see the truth of our lives that we often can't see ourselves. A single sentence in the right context at the right time can change our lives forever. A single word from someone we love and trust can change our entire mindset. As adults, we must find ways to lessen the impact of those flawed childhood lessons on us. Understanding the larger context in which we have lived our formative years shouldn't victimize us. Instead, it should give us the clarity and conviction to work on our hearts and minds.

Being born a human is an incredible privilege and our lives have tremendous possibilities. All we need is to unlearn some of what we learned from our caregivers who possibly didn't know any better. Reminiscing our childhood, now with an adult understanding of the patriarchal structure, can soothe the hurt. Stepping away and seeing fully that our elders, however wise and moral, have also lived in this flawed structure could give us some comfort. Perhaps, the biggest tool is to not take the blows of the unkind world personally. Perhaps, the biggest gift is hindsight.

The Reddy Chandelier – The Story of My Defiance and Acceptance

Contributed by Neetu Reddy, 42, Hyderabad

"I was born into an affluent, upper caste family in Hyderabad. This Reddy household, like many others, was strict and high-nosed about traditions and rules, most of which applied only to the women and girls of the family.

I have a brother, about a year younger than me, and I remember understanding quite early on that I mattered less than him. My birthdays were never celebrated; my brother's were celebrated in posh hotels with hundreds of people amidst much fanfare. He got to eat first along with my father and grandfather; I would pick up the plates and eat much later with my mother, quietly. I was controlled and disciplined, he was pampered and indulged. If he broke my dolls, pulled my hair or stole my pencils, it would be passed off as his naughtiness. If I retaliated, I would be punished for days. He had all the liberties in the world; I had strict rules and deadlines. He wasn't taught manners, discipline or polite behaviour; my every action was scrutinized and controlled. There were small things and then, there were more apparent ones; all of which started to feel unbearable as adolescence approached.

By the time I was 15, I remember feeling a deep sense of resentment that I could hardly explain to myself. I didn't question these differences with my brother, as I assumed them to be normal, but the restrictions and rules started hurting. Living up to my parents' expectation of being a quiet, homely girl was suffocating. And much like a spring held back by force, I now started pushing back.

Fuelled by repressed anger, I started clinging to defiance and rebellion to find my identity. I don't think this defiance was rooted in any newfound adolescent confidence. Instead, it still was my deep insecurities. I chose hobbies, friends and fashion specifically to rebel. I read magazines, coloured my hair and did everything that was forbidden. My rebellion meant more to me than my own well-being. I had many loud fights with my mother and became used to a deafening indifference from my father. And at the age of 19, I did the unthinkable.

In the middle of the night, I eloped and married my neighbour, about 12 years older than me. I had gone ahead and looked the dragon in the eye. I had shamed my family, something I was told was the worst possible thing to do. I felt so invisible in that big Reddy house with big chandeliers that I was desperate to be somewhere I could see myself clearly. I was so desperate for identity that I based it on my hatred and anger. I yearned for love desperately and I agreed to get married to the first person who showed the slightest trace of that.

As expected, my father cut all ties with me, something that felt quite liberating at the time, to be honest. But as the dust settled and the scandal of my wedding slowly became old news, the full meaning of my decision started emerging. In the afternoons, all alone in the new house with my in-laws, who hoped my rich father should pay for my maintenance, I missed my Amma. I felt deeply scared and utterly alone.

I knew that this marriage was a wrong decision quite early on. It was very traditional and based on a huge imbalance of power. I had seen the template of this kind of marriage between my Amma and Pappa. I hated it, and yet, I had walked straight into a similar relationship. I was financially and emotionally fully dependent on my husband. That dependence soon turned toxic, and from being joyless, the marriage became violent within a year.

Even as I lived in a relationship that was diminishing me every day, I couldn't imagine escaping. I felt compelled to stay as I had simply nowhere else to go. I hadn't been happy for years, and as the last shred of my confidence was broken, I started to quietly accept it. Every time I was abused, I meekly accepted that power came with being a man. I had rebelled against orthodox parents, but I couldn't find the strength to now fight a violent partner. The feeling of inadequacy, which I tried to escape so desperately, found its way back into my life again. The fragile sense of freedom and strength I had found started cracking. And along with it, my self-confidence nosedived.

I was close to committing suicide when I found out I was pregnant at the age of 21. As the relationship became even more violent with this news, I went out one afternoon to get rat poison to kill myself. But something stopped me; possibly the thought of being at the centre of yet another scandal. The rebellion was getting exhausting. The next day, I reached out to my Amma. After a lonely and tumultuous pregnancy, as my daughter was born, my mother secretly rekindled ties and I started mending my broken heart with her help. After a long-drawn divorce, I walked away with my 2-year-old baby from a marriage I should have never gotten into.

After years of therapy, reading, writing and introspecting, I found a way to make sense of my experiences. Now in my forties, as I remember every small detail of those formative growing-up years, I can now understand the impact those years had. My parents were not abusive, but the environment I grew up in systematically waged a war on my being. I constantly felt invalidated and unwanted, compelled to revolt — something I couldn't shake off even after decades.

As I took responsibility for my choices and mistakes, I also understood the system that shaped those choices. I started realizing that my parents were part of a system and possibly, well-intentioned. The childhood scars they left on my personality would take a lifetime to heal, but I slowly delinked their most hurtful behaviour from them as individuals. I started to not take certain things personally.

I found the perfect partner in my second husband many years later. I have a beautiful home (sans the chandeliers!) I also take care of my dad as my younger brother is settled in the US. My daughter, now almost 20 years old, is an independent, confident young girl who I smother with affection in all ways that I can. As I found a way to not take the harm done to me personally, it started to hurt a bit less. As I found the strength to forgive my parents, I finally found the strength to forgive myself."

#Prompt 1

They say we write to taste life twice, but when a part of our life is bitter, we write to spit it out. Remember moments from your childhood when you accepted something hurtful because you felt that was normal. Look back at your growing-up days and recollect some of the earliest moments when your gender became clear to you.

Now, write a letter to the person who made you realize that as a girl, you are wanted a bit less. Do you remember the person, the incident, the place? It could be a neighbour, a grandparent, a parent, a teacher or a cousin. Do you remember who introduced you to the fact that as a girl, you are entitled to a little less freedom, love or attention? Any elder who had made you feel diminished or 'less than' because you were a girl?

Write to them today with strength and candidness. Let them know that you know today, that what they chose to do then was wrong. You deserved everything that your brother, cousin or friend did. You didn't deserve the indifference; you didn't deserve those rules that only applied to you.

Do you think you can find it in yourself to forgive them? Know that by forgiving, you dismantle their power to hurt you – you dismantle their power to still be the voice in your head.

Trust that writing things down could liberate you from that unexpressed resentment and anger. Trust that it could give you the courage to accept yourself without the misplaced guilt of being born a woman.

Connect with others with similar stories on @everyday.revolution_ on Instagram.

#Prompt 2

If you have a daughter, niece, or any young girl in your life that you care for and love, write a letter to her. As an adult, now that you know how our formative childhood years affect our lives, tell her how you would make her world full of love and unbridled encouragement. Promise her that in your own way, however small, you would change this inequal world for her. How would you ensure this little girl would grow up and become a proud woman with a mind of her own and a voice of her own? How would you ensure she is protected from the gendered experience of feeling diminished at a young age?

**Share your stories with the world
@everyday.revolution_ on Instagram.**

3

Lessons in *Maryada, Sharam &* *Bipod*

The one on the fear that is taught and abandon that is left untaught

"A much elder cousin put his penis on my hands at the age of 8, when I didn't even know what a penis looked like or what it was for. I cried for days, but couldn't tell anyone."

"In our school, there was a narrow alley and a lone set of stairs that would get totally clogged when all students rushed out together during lunch or when classes got over. In the unmanageable crowd, I was groped by some boys. I didn't tell anyone, but every time the school bell rang, I used to be petrified."

"It was during a janmashthami pooja in a mandir. I was groped by someone in the crowd. I was too shocked to react; I cried alone at night for a full week."

"At the age of 12, a 30-year-old neighbour wrote an explicit letter to me about how my breasts bounced when I played badminton in the courtyard. He said he was an *admirer of my game and meant no harm. I could never play freely again without thinking of my body and how it looked."*

"A neighbourhood shopkeeper used to follow me when I walked back from my tuitions. He would make lewd gestures and sing songs loudly. I often had nightmares about him and woke up with night sweats. I started making excuses and stopped taking those classes."

"Battamizi and Chedh-chaadh by boys were common. But we were told, we shouldn't make a big fuss about it; not take panga with them. What if they get angry and throw acid on us? What if they get their gang and beat us or rape us?"

I heard the word *bipod* for the first time when I was about 5 or 6 years old. It is an all-encompassing word in Bengali, which roughly translates as danger and could mean a wide variety of things – from a minor bicycle accident to rape. It is a vague description of all the bad things that could possibly happen to me in case I was reckless. It was a useful cautionary word used by my parents whenever they didn't want to argue and explain themselves. There were other renditions of this word of caution that women hear all around: *"maryada samajh ke chalo," "aakho mein sharam rakho," "reserve ho ke raho," "zyada heehee haa haa mat karo." "Sit properly," "Cover your knees," "Be quiet; don't be loud."* It seems like the world is constantly letting us know that we live in a big bad world.

Girls are taught to grow up quickly and be conscious and cautious. We learn to be constantly on guard to save ourselves from the world. Our childhood doesn't remain carefree for very long. Our days of jumping from the trees, rolling in the mud and chasing butterflies with the boys in the neighbourhood are cut short by lessons of morals, perfection, manners and boundaries. Don't wear *badmuda*, sit this way, talk that way.

These instructions are not just for the world with strangers out there. Even in the presumable safety of our homes, we have a covert fear-mongering that tells us that we simply cannot be ourselves. We cannot be relaxed and carefree. We learn that we must choose between freedom and safety and we can't have both. Dressing properly or speaking meekly are ways of protecting us. We come to believe that our safety ultimately lies with us, even at the age when we hardly understand *what* exactly is it that we were keeping ourselves safe from.

Research says that as early as primary school, boys and girls start experiencing a different world. In pre-school, boys "shout out" answers 8 times more than girls. Girls who do shout out are told to "raise their hands and wait to be called out." While we tell girls they need to be rule-bound and careful, boys have an extended childhood which is indulged and accepted. Their free-spiritedness is cheered by their parents, teachers and neighbours. They are given space to speak, break rules, be irreverent and yet, be lovingly accepted, while girls are taught to keep themselves safe from harm, be careful and toe the line. Much of it might be un-intentional but most caregivers create a glaring difference between the childhood experiences of average boys and girls.

According to a pivotal developmental child psychology theory by Erik Erikson, as early as preschool years of 3-5 years, children start developing a sense of ambition and direction that later forms the basis of their identity. To develop a sense of confidence and initiative in their later years, children should be able to plan activities, accomplish tasks and face challenges in their early years. Parents or other influential adults like teachers and nannies who are discouraging or dismissive may cause children to develop shame and become overly dependent upon others for help and approval. We empower boys in million different ways: we cheer their bravery and tell them their lives have unlimited possibilities, we let them be soaked in dust and mud, we allow them to be out until late and we let them be naughty and break rules. This slowly-conditioned confidence sets boys up for a carefree lifetime. Similarly, the fear-infused childhood sets up girls for a cautious, unsure future.

Sadly, this advice of constant caution that girls learn isn't unjustified. World over, girls and women *are* subject to unspeakable atrocities. The *bipod* eventually does come knocking in our lives in a variety of hideous ways, mostly from within the environment which cautioned us against it. In some homes, there is physical or sexual abuse; in others, there is a *fear* of it.

When I interviewed women, it seemed everybody had a story to tell or a nightmare to share. Some experiences were physically violent and others were deeply emotionally scarring. Some attacks did not come from a physical touch but came from objectification and harassment. Little girls, who were yet to explore and understand their own bodies, became deeply conscious of it. Girls who were just starting to experience the world learnt the heinousness it is capable of instead of realizing the wonderous possibilities it holds.

And that changes a part of us forever. Some remembered resorting to baggy clothes, others to self-harm. Many seemed to have moved on. For many, wounds had healed, while for many, it really didn't. Some found closure, others buried the memories. Some internalized those experiences, while others struggled with it. There were the big traumas and then, there were the small ones. A wide range of experiences with an even wider range of responses and coping mechanisms – mostly covered in years of undue shame and guilt.

I experienced an incident of lewd touching at a bus stop at the age of 16. I don't remember the exact sequence of events, but I remember feeling an incoherent rage, much of it somehow directed towards myself. I froze for a moment, put my head down and ran back home. Despite my rather well-fuelled confidence, I couldn't scream or make a scene. I didn't follow the man or beat him up or take him to the police. I imagined doing all of this and worse in my head repeatedly for months.

Right around the same time, there was exhaustive news coverage of an incident of rape and blackmail in Ahmedabad on New Year's Eve. The whole reporting of the case focussed on the woman's character, her reckless choice of going to the party with strangers, what she wore and how late she'd stayed out. Possibly for the first time, I understood what it was like to feel weak – to feel deeply vulnerable. I understood what it was like to be attacked and wronged and yet, get no justice or closure. My personal experience and the way the world treated the girl who experienced something much worse left a big gaping dent in my carefree confidence and shook the way I looked at the world. For the first time, I saw a frightening side of the world, and I don't think I have ever been able to forget it completely.

Women feel they are at risk because they possibly are. Being born a woman is the single biggest statistical danger to the health and wellbeing of humans. Data suggests that mortal danger is lurking around women all through their lives and especially in their formative childhood years. About 60 little girls are raped in India every day according to the 2018 NCRB report. More than 90% of these rapes are committed by people known to the victim. [3]

Our homes are often worse than the big bad world we are constantly cautioned against. But these statistics simply indicate the rate of violence. But what it doesn't capture is much more sinister – the *fear* of violence. The fear of violence fundamentally changes the way women experience their lives. Through the cautionary tales that we are taught, along with our own horrific experiences, women learn something that stays with us even in safe spaces and intimate settings – fear. A nagging, ever-present and sometimes, irrational fear of being at risk.

With age, we learn to live with our fear. Stalking becomes romantic and physical abuse is justified as 'the heat of the moment.' In many ways, we learn to take the emotions and desires of men, sexual or otherwise, more seriously than our own. We learn to pacify men whenever possible. We tell them that we have a boyfriend rather than saying we're just not attracted to them. We avert all eye contact with the guy that stares at us on the bus. We obsess over our clothes; we check how we sit. And slowly but quite systemically, we are enculturated to be uncomfortable. We learn to ignore our discomfort by pushing it back and learning to live with it. We learn that we need to bear with this world, however uncomfortable, silently and without making a big fuss about it.

And many years later, conditioned for years to remain politely silent, we do remain deafeningly silent – about the unwanted dick pics, about the unfunny jokes, about the impolite advances. And then, the silence continues all through our life, be it the discomfort of awkward or boring sex or the impracticality of a wired bra or the nagging fear of being harassed on a lonely street. We remain silent.

Men in our lives, even the closest of our companions, don't truly understand this about us. They don't know that we can never not be careful and conscious. They don't know that we often can't shake off the feeling of being vulnerable even in the safest of environments. They don't understand that we never learnt to not take ourselves too seriously – to let loose and become free. We never learnt the lesson of confidence without motivational quotes and memes.

Our first instincts were not formed around encouragement and support; they were developed around caution and fear. Even as grown adult women, when we try and take a meditative, introspective walk, we worriedly look around every now and then. As a professional in a boardroom, we worry about speaking out of turn. Even in our most intimate relationship, we can never burp or laugh loudly. In homes, public spaces and even in our relationships, we are constantly fearful, deeply aware of the boundaries for our thoughts, the limits of our choices and a constant shame for our bodies. We never feel entitled to the space we occupy, often double guessing and limiting our spread throughout our lives.

Our childhood lays the foundation of many things in our lives. It takes many years for us to unpack some of the experiences we have and lessons we learn at that tender age. Our learning begins even before our formal education does. We imbibe many things without knowing the full scope and scale of their impact on our lives. While many things tend to become obsolete or impractical in our grown lives, for us women, this fear-mongering advice to be constantly cautious and distrustful does not leave us well into adulthood and much later. In the adult world, our spaces are largely occupied by loud grown men and they continue to be a testament to our imbalanced world.

But there is something I learnt across many expensive psychology courses – despite the ghastliest of memories, we can still rewire our brain. Despite heartbreaks that may have left a gaping hole in it, we can be happier. We can overcome incredible grief and we can unlearn some of the most deeply ingrained lessons. It might not look possible at present, but it becomes possible one day. And the journey starts the day we look back at our childhood experiences with gentleness and wonder. You don't remain just that one story and one version of yourself the whole life. You heal, you cope and you get closure in whatever form it might come. We can forget almost anything; we can recraft almost any part of our personality and come to a point in our lives where we look back and the hurt seems manageable if not forgettable.

Sometimes, healing might be the ability to tell some people to fuck off from our lives and sometimes, healing might mean not needing to do so anymore. Sometimes, healing means to be able to forget and sometimes, it means we never forget and ensure that nobody else goes through what we did. And despite everything, one of the oldest clichés remains true – time heals. And one of the newest clichés holds true as well – therapy works.

In our world, we teach little girls a lot of things. Way too many things, honestly. What we don't teach them is abandon. Courage and fearlessness are important and must be taught and practised, but we also should be able to teach girls abandon. It is that elusive quality of being able to just be. We need to teach little girls that they too can be adventurous, they too can seek thrill and pleasure. They are entitled to their space in the world, they are entitled to respect in the world and they are, sure as hell, entitled to safety in this world. Her freedom cannot be the price she pays for her safety when the same comes free for Men.

It might come as a shocker to many, but women are human beings. They are autonomous living beings fully worthy of their space and entitled to their choices. It's the most beautiful thing in the world when a woman speaks up against injustice at home, street or in their office. It does take one step of courage to move things – to report a street harasser or a pervert boss, to get out of an abusive relationship or to speak one's mind in a loud room.

But while we make that journey to courage for ourselves in our lives, we must take this ahead from courage to abandon for our daughters and nieces. For most of us, abandon might have to be learnt, consciously practised and may never fully replace the fear which has become such a huge part of our instinct. However, we can try to ensure that our daughters develop that carefree abandon as a default. She needs to cultivate the courage to manoeuvre this world which is filled with patronizing bosses, chauvinistic boyfriends, and vile online trolls, but she also needs to cultivate a carefree abandon to enjoy this beautiful world and explore her full potential without constantly looking over her shoulder.

Memories of Jamalpur – A Childhood Lost in Fear

By Rachita Sharma (name changed), Madrid.

While I was born and brought up in a small town in Bihar, I had a rather privileged childhood. At least for a girl. In an environment that was teeming with parents obsessed with saving adequate dowries for their daughters, I grew up in a household where academics were the only priority regardless of gender. My parents paid no heed to my grandmother's remarks about my skin colour or my broad nose with an unshakeable determination that I would either be a doctor, an engineer or an IAS officer. I turned out to be none, but that is a story for another day.

My first experience with gender expectations was when on learning that I had a kiddie crush on a boy in my class, my mother said that I should never repeat this to anyone. She clarified that a guy would never suffer any consequences if he said so, but a word of this will ruin me for life. I was barely six. This was probably why, when a year later, I was molested in class by a teacher, I never uttered a word to anyone including my parents.

Four years later, a boy in our class started harassing three girls. I was one of them. When one of the girls told her mother about this, the response was a slap, not to the boy but to the girl. I still don't know why her mother thought that was a justified response, but that was enough warning for me to never mention anything about the harassment to my mother.

Despite these experiences, when a boy from my neighbourhood, whose name I still don't know, started to stalk me incessantly when I was in eighth grade, I was so fed up that I told my parents. My parents seemed concerned but also appreciated my honesty. They promised, "We are happy that you told us. We will handle this." They added, "Just never engage with the guy in any form or manner. If he tries to talk to you, just ignore him."

I was relieved at this rather unexpectedly positive reaction and their confidence in me. For a while, I forgot all about it. Little did I know this was only the beginning of a long nightmare. When my father confronted the boy and told him that he was aware of his misconduct, instead of backing down, this prodigal stalker took it as a challenge. He was everywhere, from my school to tuitions, peeping through the windows and following me on the streets. He used to call our landline phone twenty times a day and whispered songs from the movie "Dhadkan."

I was so fed up with the constant dread that I wanted to disappear. It did not help that since I had turned 13 and had hit a sudden growth spurt, my teachers, aunts, friends and everyone around me had been reminding me of how big I was and how large and vulgar my breasts were. I still remember a full-grown man whispering to me, a fourteen-year-old, on the road, "You must be doing it with multiple men to have breasts like that." And I remember my teacher pulling me out of yoga class at school to tell me that I needed to ask my mother to buy me a bra.

Due to all this, by now, I had started to bend my gait, feeling ashamed of my body. I never participated in any form of sports, and privately, did all sorts of exercises to reduce my breast size, believing that it may be the reason I was being followed. Nothing helped, and because the stalking started getting more aggressive, my mother did what she thought was best – permanently lock all the windows in peak June during a heat wave so that no one could peep inside. This, when it was usual for our town to not receive any electricity for five to six hours, especially during summer.

I could not go to my own terrace, answer a single phone, meet my friends, attend any birthday parties, or walk twenty steps without a chaperone. Things kept getting worse over the following months and years. One of these days, my father met with this boy's father, who was surprisingly apologetic and understanding. He severely reprimanded his son in front of my father and made him promise never to bother me again. My father came home in high spirits.

However, our ease was short-lived, as the boy's mother, sister and brother visited our house the next day and started yelling, "Your daughter dances and plays on the terrace and winks at my son. She sends him letters, of which we have proof. She is the one trying to enchant him."

This was the same son whose name I never knew and the son who never once talked to me. I overheard this conversation from my room, and in my rage, picked up a kitchen knife. I have had enough. Before I could run out and hurt someone, one of my aunts stopped me and locked me in the kitchen. I sometimes wonder what could have been if she hadn't stopped me that day.

After making the accusations, they said, "Your daughter's reputation is already ruined. Why not get her married to our son? We will accept her."

I was fifteen.

Contrary to what is usual in smaller towns, the whole neighbourhood backed us. The family of the un-named stalker had to go back home as the crowd got furious.

Before leaving, however, the stalker's sister threatened, "Just remember, we know how to abduct girls."

This was the last straw for my parents. They ended up filing a police report, which was a huge deal for a middle-class home like ours. This was not for stalking, but it was put under a different pretext because apparently, my being the victim of a crime could also cause ill-repute. While the case went on and the family continued their allegations against me, my mother cried and worried incessantly.

One day, she told me, "I had a dream last night where I see that I have put you up in a place so high that no one can touch you."

Once I moved out for college, I went back to the town only once. It was like revisiting the claustrophobia, the sweaty windowless rooms and streets of dread. Even after years of leaving that place, my parents worry from time to time. Those four years were a living nightmare, but the scarier part is that things could have been much worse. We all know that acid attacks and rapes remain way too familiar and common in such small towns.

Today, far away from Jamalpur, in Madrid, I have a loving, respectful partner, a career and a tight-knit group of supportive friends, including my strong-willed, rebellious sister. But some scars remain. I constantly turn around on the streets at the slightest sound. I still have body image issues (which I have learnt to hide very well), and I have, largely unprovoked, outbursts of fury like the day I ran with a knife.

Someone asked me what would be my advice to any young girl in my position, I have just one piece of advice for her – let no one make you believe for a second that any of it is your fault. But the real advice is to the society. Stop defending the criminal. Stop blaming the victim. Stop shaming girls. This nightmare that I lived through for years would have been nipped in the bud had there been no secrecy and fear of public prosecution. And I too, could have had a childhood with happy, carefree memories.

#Prompt 3

1. Those moments that you have felt unsafe and harmed in the past…are you ready to write about those troubling memories? Do you think you can find it in yourself to put that experience in words? In writing about upsetting events, there might come a new understanding of the events. It might free you from the misplaced sense of responsibility you felt for those experiences. Problems that seem overwhelming might become somewhat manageable after you see them on paper. In some way, writing about haunting experiences might help resolve them in some way. It's worth giving it a try.

2. Imagine a time when you walked freely on the street. I am asking you to be reckless, free and unhinged, even if it's only on the paper or in your head! Imagine a space of freedom. Imagine walking to the nearest market alone on a windy night to buy your favourite chocolates. Imagine you can cycle your way around the whole city, sit at a *dhaba* at 5 A.M and have chai while you listen to your favourite song. Imagine you can sleep under the stars on a beach, read on a bench in a park, run on empty roads, stop in the middle of a highway to watch a sunset, stay outside all night and watch a sunrise — just exist freely and safely without fear. I am trying for you to know abandon, even if it is for a moment. I want you to seek your space in this world. Now, imagine what clothes would you

wear, how would you walk and who would you be with. Free yourself from the fear of harm; see how that would be for you. Practice that fearlessness in your mind and you would see that it might come alive in your life.

Practice this abandon in your life. Slowly and steadily, bring that freedom into your daily life. Abandon needn't be only on a night out there on the street. Abandon could come in the way we approach our lives – our jobs, relationships and bodies. Fear manifests itself in our lives. Fearlessness works similarly.

Share your stories with other women and find solidarity, connection and comfort @everyday. revolution_on Instagram

4

Growing Up in a Binary World of *Mard* and *Aurat*

The one about learning the rules and roles of the gender binary

"'Papa ke paise gol-gol, Mummy ki Roti gol-gol' was a couplet we used to sing along as kids."

"In our north Indian culture, men who do household work are called 'Mehra.' I have heard that in the Western Indian cultures, they are called 'Bayla.' When we were growing up, women giggled and gossiped about men who would cook or do housework and called them these names."

"I was a complete tomboy growing up. I loved to play outdoors and race with the boys. I remember being schooled and shamed for it by relatives and neighbours. I gradually gave up."

Like oxygen, dust and patriarchy, my parents have always been around, a part of my life and a part of who I am. I must tell you; my parents were incredible. From patience to tact, sense of humour to resilience – much of what I am or claim to be, was knowingly or unknowingly taught by them. They were hustlers who tried their best to provide for everything their daughters needed.

When we were kids, I remember that Baba travelled extensively for his job. His job always looked powerful and important. When he was at home, he had the best piece of fish served on the biggest plate we had. He drove the car, managed our monies and planned our vacations. My Ma, on the other hand, was homely, devoted, and dutiful. She seemed to be fully responsible for our school, homework, tiffin, clean nails, tantrums, manners and more. She had a full-time job, but her job seemed somewhat disposable when we were sick or needed her to come for PTAs. There was a running joke when we were growing up that Baba didn't know how old we two sisters were or what grade we were in at school. It seemed very funny to everyone then. It doesn't any more to me.

Psychologists have proven in many ways that a child's earliest exposure to what it means to be male or female comes from their parents and not from within their bodies. Multiple research and books on intersex patients have helped explain how social factors are much more important than biological factors in gender identity and gender roles. Researchers suggest that by the age of 2-3, children start to become aware of their sex – whether they are male or female and come to understand that there are these two distinct types of people in this world.

It is between 4 and 6 years of age that a boy will realize he will grow up to be a man, much like his father and a girl comes to understand that she will become a woman like her mother. It is around this age that they start looking for clues in the behaviour of their parents to try and replicate that in their behaviours. Cross-cultural studies reveal that children are aware of gender roles by age two or three, and at four or five, most children are firmly entrenched in culturally appropriate gender roles (Kane, 1996). They start understanding what is appropriate for each gender. What parents do, their equation with each other and what they expect of us is possibly the first time the performance of gender is observed, understood, and imbibed in us.

Then comes the explicit ways kids are treated by their parents. From the time their children are babies, parents treat sons and daughters differently, dressing them differently, giving them different toys and even expecting different behaviours. A study done in 2002 showed that parents have different expectations from sons and daughters as early as 24 hours after birth! [4] From infancy, mothers use more facial expressions when speaking to female babies and use more emotional words in conversation with them as they get older. Parents offer the male children trucks, toy guns, Lego, pirate costumes and racing cars with steroid-infused men on the boxes and illustrated in supposedly manly colours of blue and black. And in contrast, female children are often given dolls with miniature heels, princess outfits, tea sets and dress-up apparel. The toys for the boys are largely active toys that promote motor skills, aggression and solitary play. The toys for girls foster nurturing skills, social proximity and roleplay. This indoctrination into gender is insidious and powerful in the lives of malleable, impressionable children. Studies have shown that children will most likely choose to play with "gender appropriate" toys even when cross-gender toys are available because parents give children positive feedback (in the form of praise, involvement and physical closeness) for gender-normative behaviour. [5]

Children come into a gendered world. Most of us, having been brought up by heterosexual parents, have grown to accept a template of gendered love and work. Most of our parents have lived all their lives according to their gender, and through their lessons, they pass this on to the next generation. This means an ongoing cycle of gendered expectations. Once gender is set, it is set in us for life. We have a template to live by. The ideas we learn about appropriate behaviour based on gender are not like instincts that we are wired with. They are communicated by education, inculcated by family and reinforced by pop culture.

We are socialized via four major agents: family, education, peer groups and mass media. Each agent reinforces gender roles by creating and maintaining normative expectations for gender-specific behaviour. Exposure also occurs through religion and the workplace. Repeated exposure to these agents over time leads people into a false sense that they are acting naturally rather than following a socially constructed role. We end up thinking it is only natural to behave according to these man-made gender norms.

We believe that the differences between boys and girls in terms of preferences and behaviour are endowed in the womb. As we grow to identify what is "normal," "good" or "right," our brains start leaning on stereotypes to judge the normalcy or acceptability of ours and other people's behaviours. As adults, we may theoretically understand the social nature of gender or learn that it is not biology but a social construct, but we continue to expect those who identify as women or men to act in accordance with their gender.

It is only now that I fully understand the incredible harm we do when we have deeply gendered parenting in our lives. When we see distinct and templatized roles our mom and dad play in our lives, we set up a life that follows a similar diktat. I know I have deeply internalized these roles myself. Our flawed education system makes us good at learning what is being taught. But it doesn't make us good at arriving at what we think. It often doesn't equip us to form our own opinions. It has taken me many years to realize that I am meant to think, meant to be self-critical, meant to be combative, meant to question the status quo and never just accept something without evaluating and analysing it with the might of my own mind.

But I have never fully been able to objectively look at my Ma and Baba's actions. I can so easily find love and empathy for them, which I often find inaccessible for nameless people. Even when I look at their flawed and gendered parenting, my resentment is mixed with patience. My judgements are often softened by the understanding that they were so much more than their shortcomings. The rigidity of the gender binary is how they had lived their lives and known the world. As I now have the language and tools to look at my parents' actions and my memories, I also learn to have subjectivity and empathy to look at the behaviour of others. And I know that people are an outcome of the world they lived in.

Conditioning is everything. It defines what we know of the world and defines who we are. Our favourite music, favourite cuisine, and favourite political candidate are all outcomes of conditioning. Much like the laws of gravity, the laws of conditioning or learning are also constantly in action. We learn by association, we learn by experience, we learn by repetition. And gender is one of the most deeply embedded constructs in our world; it's one of the most common axes upon which our life experiences can be plotted. It is the primary way in which we arrange our social world. It's the thing we register the first and fastest when we meet someone. It is everywhere – what is acceptable behaviour, what is acceptable clothing, what are acceptable life choices; everything is soaked and marinated for generations in this construct of gender.

Bem Sex-Role Inventory (BSRI), a survey developed in the 1970s, is still referred to in many gender studies across the globe. This was designed by Sandra Bem to evaluate the extent to which people aligned themselves to the cultural definitions of gender. The test asks some uncomfortable, single-worded questions and gives you a score which makes you stare at the screen for a few minutes. But the important thing that BSRI has been able to disprove is this belief that if an individual did not behave as expected of their gender, it was a sign of poor mental health. The belief that unless we neatly fit into feminine values as a female and squarely masculine values as a man, we won't live peaceful, well-adjusted lives in this world. The test using empirical evidence has been able to prove that gender roles could be fluid and that both sexes could embody the opposite gender's traits and, in fact, this fluidity is the healthier state being. BSRI surveys have proven conclusively that more balanced people are those who are able to incorporate both feminine and masculine behaviours and they may actually be happier and more well-adjusted than those who are strongly sex-typed as either masculine or feminine. As a corollary, it proves that following the rigid binary structure of gender that is prescribed by society is potentially harmful to our wellbeing. One in five women are more "male-like" than the average man. Overall, there is enough scientific evidence and millions of people's lived experiences to tell us that gender is a spectrum, and we all fall somewhere on that scale of masculine and feminine identities.

The binary construct of gender in our world is violent, even if it might not be physically violent to all. It is enforced with an invisible militancy. Along with being a system that templatizes human behaviours, it creates unimaginable violence in homes and streets. The performance of this rigid binary system is often emotionally and psychologically scarring. As women repress their "masculine" side and men repress their "feminine" side, we chip away a part of our truest selves and comply with vague ideals of appropriate behaviours. World over, this construct creates oppressive environments for everyone –

heterosexual men, women and queer folks of all types of gender expressions.

Of course, women and gender-binary non-conforming folks are immensely disadvantaged in this patriarchal world, but the gender construct also boxes heterosexual men into emotional stoicism that has been very strongly linked to a higher range of mental health issues. Good boys don't cry; good boys never show vulnerability. That's exactly how good boys end up becoming deeply troubled and profoundly unhappy grown men.

Many generations of Feminist revolution have redefined womanhood; women are taught they can be anything (at least the privileged ones like myself). But even the privileged men didn't have a similar movement which told them they could be anything they wanted to be. They could stay at home and take care of the kids. They could like fashion more than football without getting ousted from their macho scotch-drinking circles. Most men, therefore, are still locked into the same rigid, outdated model of masculinity.

But even if we allow women to be a tad bit masculine or men to be slightly feminine, we are very careful about its overreach. The permission we get from our society to go even slightly beyond the set templates of the gender binary is only temporary. We don't let people be unless they come back into the fold of the binary and neatly fit into one box or the other.

We have all seen the pre-interval Anjali in *Kuch Kuch Hota hai*. She wasn't like other girls, she hated to be called a girl. Implicit in her "*eww* I am not a girl" was a disdain for the feminine traits of dress-up and make-up and an awe for all things manly and rugged. Many women claim to have been a tomboy when they were younger. They naturally found more in common with the boys. Boys seemed to be more interesting and fun and got appreciated for things other than their appearances. They loved that. And much like Anjali, tomboyish girls often find themselves becoming popular. But despite her popularity and confidence, there was one thing Anjali wasn't – desirable. She couldn't simply be herself to be loved. She had to disappear, grow her hair, change the way she walked, put on make-up, wear a sari and get 100% *shuddh desi* feminine to be liked by the man who remained a child forever.

And much like our neighbourhood aunty, this movie told us subtly that we can have our androgynous traits; we may play sports or drink beer or love video games. These are allowable girl traits, but a real woman needs to leave all of this behind and transform into a femme goddess to be loved.

Embracing ourselves means embracing all sides of us. Knowing that people can have a beard, muscular forearm and a penis and yet, be deeply nurturing and motherly. One can be ambitious and yet, be interested in making *Rangoli* or knitting scarfs. When we stop bracketing jobs, personalities, clothes and habits is when we allow people to be their true selves without the diktats of gender.

Growing up in this binary world could be confusing and limiting for most boys and girls, but it is particularly brutal to the ones who do not conform to the binary. The kids who don't fit into these categories are told that they are wrong. From the androgynous girl to a sari-wearing little boy, we tell these kids who dare to explore their identities beyond what is so forcefully taught to them, that they are not real. We ridicule them and punish them until they conform. We define these brackets of male and female not so much by what they are but by what they are not. This fear that people project on kids or adults who identify as queer, trans, intersex or gay is actually a phobia against uncertainty and exploration. Because any questioning of gender breaks open our hard-wired understanding of this world. Once we acknowledge the experience of queer, gender-non-conforming kids, we acknowledge that most of what we have based our own identities and personalities on is a fantasy. We realize that we have modelled our whole lives based on what we *should be like* and not on who we truly are.

No one is born with gender literacy. We are born into families that teach us what it means to be a man or a woman, and that there are just those two options. But it is the non-confirming people who struggle with an identity in this world, who find it difficult to neatly fit in despite the boxes being so violently offered to them, who show us that exploration is possible. They teach us that it is possible to learn and question. They teach us that we don't need to repress our instincts. And that those are the greatest joys of being alive and being human.

It is through those who do not subscribe to the gender binary that we get an insight into the way we can re-arrange this world beyond the two neat boxes. Because it is they who are able to see what we can't. It is through the different reality of their anatomy that gender non-binary people find insight into unpacking the gender roles and seeing the problems in them. It is through their different reality that they can find the courage to shake up these rules and roles that the rest of us accept and then, contort and contour ourselves to fit into. We cover up the contradictions within ourselves instead of dissecting them and dis-empowering them because we think gender is an unshakeable framework. Those who identify as gender fluid or non-binary give us a window into an alternate life. They show us what someone would look like if they had the courage to live a life without pressing down their natural instincts.

While this world could be incredibly harsh to those who are trans, queer, gay, or gender-fluid, it is in their exploration and curiosity that we have a window to our liberation from the suffocating boxes of being gender binary. It is through their experience that we realize that we are born free people in the 21st century and can express ourselves whichever way we want. It is through accepting and loving those who dare to question the gender binary that we can imagine a world where boys can be vulnerable, girls can be loud and the ones who do not identify very neatly as either can be whatever the hell they want to be. And it doesn't necessarily need us to erase the template of man and woman but to simply acknowledge that these identities could be what we make of them and these two identities are just two out of the many.

#Prompt 4

1. For most of us, the gender binary is unquestioned and deeply embedded in our daily lives. One of the ways to dismantle that construct and to somewhat free us from it is to look back at our lives actively through the lens of gender.

   As a woman, reminisce how you internalized the way your mom was treated in your home. What part of her life are you reliving that you would rather not? Is there a cycle you feel you have continued? Is there a way you could now discontinue it for your children?

2. Remember what it felt like to be divided into two groups on the playground and never have the option of going over to the other side. When did you learn what it was to be a girl? When did you learn what being a "good girl" was? What do you think is the most cumbersome part of being a woman? What part of being a woman feels like a "performance" to you that takes energy and effort?

3. Remember the cultural icons we were told to worship, the dolls and the books we were given. Did you resonate with these stories and fables naturally? Did any of this feel wrong at the time? If you had to re-create them, what would the dolls and heroines for your daughter look like?

Share your stories with other women and find solidarity, connection and comfort @everyday.revolution_on Instagram.

Marriage

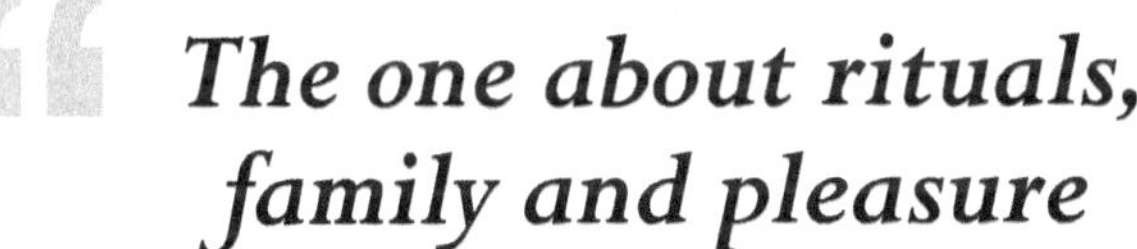

5

Shadi – The Problem in the Recipe

*The one on Marriage — its unmissable charm and
structural flaws*

*"I am a Hindu, and I dated a Christian boy in college,
my first serious relationship. We were so crazy in love. He
had talked about our relationship with his parents and they
were hysterically opposed to this match. I never even told my
parents. We simply walked away from each other when the
course ended and never looked back. I sometimes wonder
what my life could have been with him."*

*"I am 31 and my mom and dad have been trying to
find a match for me from matrimony.com for the last 4 years.
Somehow, things are simply not working out. I am starting to
feel there is something wrong with me."*

*"I am 42 and I have lost count of the number of men I
have met through sites, aunties and apps. My lasting memory
of my thirties is desperately trying to lose weight, getting
dressed to meet some man in a restaurant and then, seeing it
fall through."*

"I go on dates through Bumble and Tinder, but I will need to close the deal soon. I just turned 30. I don't think I have a lot of time to just go on dates. Men have more time."

When I married Aditya in 2015, in a Bengali-Gujrati hybrid ceremony, it didn't exactly feel very normal. Even if we had known each other for about 7 years, we still felt awkward, nervous and unsure. There were tons of photographers who were running around the two of us as if their entire lives depended on getting the 'candid' pictures that were entirely orchestrated. I was constantly worried about getting the right angle on camera that suitably hid my arm fat. Aditya was worried about his slipping *Dhoti*, which he somehow thought was the bigger problem. The whole rigmarole was chaotic with the whole family getting dressed in jarringly shiny clothes, fussing over the Garam Masala in the Dal while my parents seemed to be getting dangerously close to a panic attack.

I imagine 5000 years ago, when the first recorded marriage happened, it was far less of a fuss. Anthropologists believe that for thousands of years before that, families were simply a group of up to 30 people, with male leaders and multiple women and children shared by them. The advent of marriage was primarily to bind women to men, guaranteeing that a man's children were his biological heirs. It was a brilliant invention that ensured that the only thing which women controlled – birthing children – was kept firmly within the sphere of male control. One of the fundamental principles of marriage was to make the woman and her children a man's property. Etymologically, the word "husband" literally comes from the agricultural term animal husbandry. We might want to remember this etymological origin of the word the next time we coyishly introduce our husband.

Surprisingly, the ownership of women by their husbands is still an actual assumption in many laws and penal codes across many countries. The doctrine of Coverture, a legal principle in common law, adapted by many countries worldwide in at least some form, states that a woman is not a separate legal entity after marriage and is consumed within the legal rights of her husband. The bride gives up her name to symbolize the surrendering of her identity and the husband becomes the official public representative of two people, not one.

IPC Section 497 that penalizes adultery in India assumes that having intercourse with another man's wife is akin to trespassing on his property and had a commensurate punishment. It is worth remembering that in the not-so-distant history, a woman had no separate legal rights. Legal rights, mind you – not a social convention or informal rituals – legal, constitutional, basic rights as citizens.

In terms of social symbols, the basic premise of the Hindu wedding rituals, *Kanyadan* of the bride or the promises made during the *Saat Pheras*, is based on the assumption that the groom is the new guardian or owner of the bride. Implicit in the photo-worthy ritual of *Vidai,* i.e., the giving away of the bride, is an obvious de-prioritization of a woman's autonomy, her identity and her parents. It might be uncool to say it out loud, but the remnants of that grotesque, archaic principle that assumed women to be less of a person than the man she marries remains widely hidden in plain sight in our *instagrammable* rituals even today. For women, how so ever we gloss over it, diverting our attention to our saree or make-up, the fancy weddings we spend most of our childhood dreaming of, basically legitimizes our inequal, disadvantaged place in this pivotal relationship of our lives.

Feminist rage against the institution of marriage is, therefore, not entirely devoid of merit. The institution of marriage has, for thousands of years, been one of the most powerful instruments of oppression – governing women's bodies, autonomy, choices and more. They say marriages are often the truest testament of patriarchy, somewhat of a litmus test. If one must see how inequal a society is, one could just observe 100 marriages in it closely. Indian parents from affluent, urban homes, get their girls educated, make them independent, and encourage them to work. But all freedoms and choices eventually end with marriage, which absolutely must be caste/religion/class/age-appropriate.

Many millennial women I met talked about this suddenly contradicting, rather awkward change they observed in their otherwise cool parents when they approached the marriageable age. Seemingly progressive parents, who have their girls study, read and travel, suddenly become hopelessly conventional when it comes to marriage. All freedoms, all indulgences seemed to end for women as they near the small window of *shadi* age.

Looking back, I am somewhat embarrassed by my own enthusiastic compliance with the problematic convention of marriage. Why did I voluntarily agree to it at a rather conventional age of 27? To be honest, at the time, it didn't feel like a choice any more than it is a choice to put on clothes every day before leaving the house. I have grown up in a world where everyone was married. The ones who weren't were gossiped about and sympathized with. I can't delink my decision to get married from the barrage of pro-marriage signals I have received all my life.

Now in my 30s, I have somehow found a way to protect myself against parental and societal pressures, although I can't deny they still have inexplicable power. It's not easy to delink ourselves from the world. Despite hearing cautionary tales of unhappy marriages, despite education and access, despite feminist thoughts, the conditioning is difficult to break away from.

I have been taught to look at marriage as precious and sacred. I have grown up reading romantic fiction and planning my grand wedding for many years. When I fell in love at the age of 20, I didn't realize I would so thoughtlessly follow the trajectory of marriage as the end goal of love. But it felt like a rite of passage into adult life. Once married, we seemed like responsible people, proper adults!

But while getting married did make my visa applications and house-rent agreements easier, it also made me see patriarchy up close. I saw a gendered division of responsibilities and a blatantly different set of rules for the man and the woman. I married the man I loved and yet, we hustle every day to make this marriage equal. I have learnt that there are design flaws in the software of marriage that needs constant upgrades and reboots to make it work.

Like most things in life, there is also a deep class and caste divide in how people experience their marriages. 45% of the Indian state is categorized as middle class, roughly similar 45% have internet access, but fewer than 5% of Indians choose their own partners and even lesser than that are inter-caste marriages. The rest of the 95% of marriages are arranged and by default, caste appropriate.

Gujarati NRIs living in the US gloat about their cross-cultural celebrations when they spend Eid with their Pakistani neighbours or Christmas with their black colleagues, but when it comes to marriage, they are taught to stay away from BMW (Blacks, Muslim and Whites). Pew research has shown that among Asian-Americans, Indians have the lowest rate of inter-racial marriage with just one-in-eight Indians married to other racial/religious identities. [10]

What this indicates is obvious. For all our progressiveness, for all our Bollywood movies that show love and romance as a pre-requisite for marriage, a vast majority of Indians eventually marry in ways that reinforce the caste divide in our communities. As Dr BR Ambedkar said, the real remedy of the caste menace is inter-marriage and by corollary, the real cause of the caste system is the construct of marriage. We are steeped in this construct of caste-appropriate marriages and we know that most romantic relationships won't be able to bear the burden that comes with revolting against this template.

My wedding was dramatically unusual for the Purkayastha household. I was the first one in my family, by one account, the first one in seven generations, who was marrying a non-Bengali boy. As one can imagine, the melodrama leading up to the wedding was almost as spicy as the mustard fish served at the wedding. Thankfully, by the age of 27, I had a job in Mumbai, away from home, which gave me huge leverage in the negotiations with my parents. Also, Aditya ticked all the other boxes of being Hindu, upper-caste and Ivy-league educated. I am not sure if things would have been as smooth if these essential criteria were not met.

Most women in India don't love or even know their husbands before they get married. In some cultures, they are married off to their blood relatives, mostly much older than them. Millions of women have far more pressing issues during their wedding compared to the arm-fat conundrum I had to endure. However, the cynical data junkie in me is not entirely averse to the theoretical idea of arranged marriage. Like any other legal contract, however regressive, one does need an objective evaluation of the contract's modalities, future prospects and dissolution risks.

Much of human history has operated in a similar fashion, the idea of love as a reason for marriage only goes as far back as about a hundred years. The frailties of the human mind – cognitive bias or judgement discrepancy – are exacerbated by deep brown eyes or sexy deep voice and could potentially compromise our ability to be objective. Even for the women with limitless choices, marrying for love could be confusing and ultimately, lead to a buyer's remorse.

In this world of right-swipes, there is always someone funnier, better looking and kinder. The possibilities are endless and excruciatingly exhausting. So, meeting someone random and having our well-meaning parents make a well-informed judgement about who we might be most compatible with for a long-term relationship is *theoretically* not the worst idea. Having the finality of a legal contract which ends our double guessing of "he loves me or loves me not" also frees us up for other bigger, better purposes in life.

This idea of arranged marriage seems absurd to our western counterparts. To them, the idea of marrying someone without going through the years of confusion, insecurities, and sexual power-play that goes behind modern dating, is unbelievable. But for many of us who have grown to see long-term arranged marriages of our parents somehow work, romantic love has not proven any more effective than *janam patri* in determining the success of a relationship. For us, it makes total sense to voluntarily sign up for the mobile version of matrimony. com.

The real human *bhasad,* beyond logic, begins when the negotiations in the arranged marriage process start. Men and women face confidence-shaking rejections and self-doubt-generating taunts during the process of scrutiny that is an integral part of arranged marriages. The prospective grooms are somewhat shielded by the well-fed position of power they hold in society and this potential relationship. But most women come to witness a system of objectification and judgement. Many of these arranged marriages begin with unhealthy ego tussles, unfair demands and a clear, undeniable inequality between the *ladke-wale* and the *ladki-wale*.

The hierarchy within a marriage is reinforced in many overt and subtle ways. Women are supposed to be shorter, a bit naive, pure and slightly helpless almost in a cutesy way that feeds into a man's ego and makes him the unsaid protector or guardian.

The man is supposed to earn more than the woman, he should be from the same or better caste. He should usually be 2-3 years older and 1-2 inches taller. These templates are so well-entrenched that divergence from these norms is statistically rare and often makes the marriage a topic for lifelong gossip and taunts in social circles. In many ways, heterosexual marriages are not accidentally inequal; they are *designed* to be a relationship between two inequal entities.

But people are getting married all the time. They are also staying put in marriages for most of their lives. It is one of the most universal human experiences, a big part of most of our adult lives. Marriage is not just an institution; it is also symbolic. It is a long-standing tradition which has formed the basis of our civilization and has been one of the major tenets of our culture. In many ways, it has gotten us where we are today as a species, howsoever doomed we might be.

A feminist critique of marriage is almost out of fashion in today's world of Netflix wedding specials and Sabyasachi Lehengas. For all our options, a majority of young people still follow a similar trajectory of marriage in their twenties and having kids in their thirties. For all our wokeness and social media activism, we continue to *want* to get married.

Despite its historical, etymological and legal flaws, marriage has been proven to be good for our health and wellbeing by several years of research from across the fields of human development, psychology, neuroscience and medical science.

From a psychological standpoint, a committed relationship that offers emotional support and a common social context of meaningful shared relationships and experiences is a solid contributor to our happiness. Committed marriages also have better health benefits than simple cohabitation or live-in.

But most studies have shown that the positives of marriage impact men far more than women. A recent study by behavioural Scientist Paul Dolan shows that men benefit disproportionately more from heterosexual marriage because they calmed down, took lesser risks, earned more money and lived longer. [6] [7] Married men are also viewed as more responsible and stable by their employers and are more likely to be offered a promotion. [8]

Married women, on the other hand, are no better off than unmarried women. They die sooner than if she never married. In fact, the healthiest and happiest population subgroup are women who never married or had children. Women who get married are likely to be viewed with distrust by their employers as it is assumed that they will soon start having babies, go on maternity leave and prioritize children over work. [8] There have been multiple consistent findings that men derive more benefit from marriage, both in terms of morbidity and mortality compared to women.

It, therefore, becomes important to observe the different roles the institution of marriage plays in the lives of men and women. In a variety of different ways, marriages are made to define women's lives far more than that of men. Jennifer Aniston, Mamta Bannerjee or Rekha, we can't imagine women's lives to be happy and complete without a partner. A married woman is deemed worthy of respect and dignity and the single ones are worthy of at best pity and at worst, moral questioning. The saddest possible life one can imagine for an adult woman is if she is widowed or divorced. Women's accomplishments are considered inadequate till they have also ticked the box of marriage. These things are not true of men (case in point – Narendra Modi and Salman Khan).

For women, marriage isn't just a social construct; successful relationships are deeply linked to their perceived self-worth. Girls are taught that a husband is a form of validation and a measure of the success of their lives. Their growing up years go into preparing to be the chosen one by the man of their dreams. Many studies corroborate that the expectation of a perfect partner and believing that this one relationship will bring them all the happiness they deserve severely hampers women's well-being in the long run. [7]

There is also a different psychological and emotional approach men and women have towards marriages. Women go into a marriage for the marriage – to her, marriage itself has intrinsic, symbolic value over and above her equation with her partner. For men, the stakes are much lower and marriage itself doesn't have as much intrinsic value. Men's lives are not defined by marriage. This leads to an asymmetrical emotional involvement by men and women in this mutual contract.

This lop-sidedness presents itself in many overt and covert ways in our marriages and we are often unable to unpack it. This disproportionate expectation women set for themselves from marriage and romantic relationships does us no good at all. We are unable to see how we are simply more invested in this construct than our partners. It lays the foundation for some of our very problematic handling of incompatible relationships and often leads to the fatal mistake of choosing to remain in a relationship even when we are not loved or respected in it.

Women learn that in love, they must compromise. She is taught that to be in any relationship is to sacrifice her own well-being to cater to the needs of others. It's not that love is bad. Relationships could be one of the most profound experiences of our lives. The staunchest revolutionaries amongst us wouldn't deny its power. There is incredible beauty in companionship. But successful relationships are eventually give-and-take. Relationships do need work. Maintaining love is an everyday effort. We do need to bear with the flaws and the warts of the people we love. To be in any long-term relationship, we often need to overlook some of the flaws and shortcomings. To be able to nurture a broken heart, to be a part of someone's life in a meaningful way, needs a bit of selflessness. And all of it could be tremendously rewarding.

But we also need to cultivate an ability to know when a relationship is not nurturing or nourishing us but is depleting us of our agency, well-being and self-worth. Sacrifice and compromise shouldn't be celebrated and praised. Rather, they are things that need to be examined. Manipulation, control and abuse can never be signs of love. We must reject the movies and relatives that tell us so. Successful relationships are an equilibrium and we must develop self-awareness and self-love to gauge the *bahi-khata* of our major relationships. We must know if the relationship is tallying. This model of self-sacrificial and glorious love is not taught to men in the same way. And that's how love becomes a weapon of patriarchy to extract disproportionate, unilateral emotional labour from women in relationships.

This form of love is taught to us all our lives. We women grow up to be pathetic suckers for romance. Girls grow up dreaming of a wedding on the beach with their prince charming, with tasteful flowers and magical décor, while boys grow up in a parallel world wanting to be Batman. The genre of romantic fiction feeds on female vulnerability – that desperate want of living up to our childhood fairy tales. It glamorizes one true soulmate and makes us think marrying him is the greatest story of our lives.

The unquestioned pedestalisation of the institution of marriage makes it immune to any evaluation of its utility. The religious and social interaction that makes this one relationship in our lives morally and culturally more valuable than all others further deepen its impact on our lives. It's devastatingly misleading to expect that "the one" can single-handedly make us live happily ever after. There is, of course, no problem with dreaming of romance; what harms us is when we let the responsibility of our wellness lie on a singular relationship. What makes us perilously vulnerable is when we define our whole existence and life's purpose by another person.

Girls from affluent, educated backgrounds voluntarily leave their jobs, move cities and become a different person within a couple of months of marriage. We start to value this one relationship with our husband and the others that come with it and forget the rest. The other relationships almost become frivolous and inessential — no more important than a hobby. We are instantly supposed to "belong" to this new environment and take on these new relationships, whether or not we like it. As a woman, if you're getting married thinking you'll never be lonely again, think again, because marriage is designed to be isolating! It separates us from friends and communities and forces us to make new ones. Post-marriage depression amongst women is a widespread phenomenon that women and people around them often bury by calling it the "adjustment phase." Marriage entitles us to law-mandated companionship and commitment, but in many ways, it makes us lonelier than ever. [9]

At 27, I didn't fully understand what I was getting into when I got married. Much like my engineering degree, I only started to see its value and its redundancy much later. It is not surprising that a patriarchal construct like marriage benefits men more than women, especially because it was never institutionalized keeping us women in mind. Howsoever we eventually agree to get married – arranged, love or the recently popular 'arranged love' from matrimony sites – we need psychological digging to check what the relationship is bringing to our life.

We need to interrogate ourselves and find ways to make this ubiquitous contract work for us. Those glossy, colourful scrapbooks we had used to plan our weddings should be rightfully replaced by journals and books which push us to make our marriage nourishing for us. As human beings, we are wired for attachment, but we cannot base our life on someone else. We might realize this when it is too late, or we might realize this suddenly on a Tuesday afternoon that we are truly alone in this universe. We need to be our own person. These relationships are the surround sound in our life's symphony which makes the music beautiful. We are the lead vocalist in our life.

As the funny Indian adage goes, marriage is indeed like a big ghee-rich *laddoo*. Forgive me for stretching the metaphor, but marriages could be nourishing as well as tasty, much like the laddoo. What matters is to be able to see it for what it is and see if it has utility in our lives. It might sound simplistic, but the day we are finally able to redefine what marriages mean in our society, see it for what it truly is – two people, irrespective of gender, committing to each other – many of our prejudiced constructs for caste, class, heteronormativity will be shaken up. And while we do that, let's always remember, the laddoo is never the main course and a singular relationship can never be the core of our identity.

Fuck Soulmates – The Story of Giving Up on One True Love

Anonymous (based on the life of a very dear friend)

Varsha was super tall, curly-haired, gawky and hopelessly unaware of how attractive she was. Boys in the class would constantly try and get her attention but she simply never got the hint. She had grown up watching romantic movies and couldn't wait to meet her soulmate. But the unimpressive, flirtatious classmates just didn't live up to the mental image of her perfect future life partner.

At home, Varsha had a textbook typical set of Punjabi parents. Affluent and loud. Amidst that, how she grew up to be quiet and somewhat shy was kind of a mystery. Maybe, in the loud household where everyone wanted to speak, someone just needed to listen. Varsha was always that someone.

When she was around the age of 25, her parents signed her up at Punjabi and NRI matrimony websites and told every fufa, bua, chachi, mami, masi to look for a suitable match for her. At the time, Varsha was studying, with plans to pursue her higher education and do an MBA, but at 25, she was told she had run out of time and that she could pick it up if her future husband was OK with it after marriage. Varsha reluctantly agreed, and thus began the drama of the great Indian arranged marriage.

With the initial months came the first set of rejections. She was a bit too tall for some, a bit too dark for others. The dark circles under her eyes that she hadn't noticed before were apparently a problem. She was told that her back was hunched in the wrong way and her hair needed to be straightened. This was the first time Varsha faced such vicious objectification.

Every rejection disappointed her parents and reduced Varsha's self-belief. She started physio for her posture and keratin treatment for her hair. She never took a lot of interest in make-up or clothes before, but it now seemed almost mandatory. Varsha took up all of these with the discipline and practicality of college exams. To her, being able to get married also seemed like an exam she had to pass.

One of the prospective suitors, after the first couple of months of this drama, ticked the basic check by parents in terms of class and caste and reached the advanced level in this process. The advanced level was simply that the to-be bride and grooms meet for the first time. Unfortunately, while the checklist was all ticked, the guy was simply boring and dull. Varsha couldn't sustain a conversation beyond a couple of sentences and couldn't find anything common to talk about. After a couple of attempts, she gave up and told her parents that she didn't want to go ahead with this alliance. As a naïve entrant into this drama of arranged marriage, Varsha was surprised to know that not having chemistry wasn't an acceptable reason for a girl to reject a match.

Possibly for the first time, she saw the rage of her dad. She said he looked at her as if she had ruined his life. He seemed unreasonable and cold-blooded. All hell broke loose at home. Amidst this chaotic time, Varsha's health started suffering and she had a massive bout of panic attacks and blackouts. Her hospitalization finally ended the conversation with this suitor, but Varsha's parents made it clear that they were running out of patience.

Rebellion has its own fatigue, and fighting against one's parents can be devastatingly exhausting. As she went along the arranged marriage process, and as every rejection she faced created days of turmoil in the household, her expectations and standards kept getting lower. She started off imagining a perfect match, a guy she will fall in love with along the process, but by the time she met her future husband, she practically just wanted a guy who would agree to marry her and end this exhausting process.

Polite and progressive, her future husband left a good first impression when she met him almost a year into the search. As Varsha didn't see any reason to say no, her father immediately formalized the ceremony of "shagan" in a week's time. During the next 6 months, as Varsha excitedly planned her wedding, she found out that this polite guy could be quite emotionally charged up and unstable. But she convinced herself that he was possibly just passionate in love.

She was shocked to learn that the guy's father had a criminal record but she was convinced by her relatives that it was just something that was part of running a business. Things that even a little background check on the family could have revealed much earlier were discovered much later. And worst of all, just 10 days before the wedding, the man revealed, almost nonchalantly, that he was diabetic. For Varsha, this information felt like a deal-breaker and she was devastated, but when she mentioned this to her mom, she was told to just focus on getting married and not to share this with anyone else.

Varsha eventually did get married to this man, knowing fully well the kind of adjustments and compromises she would be required to make. But even with all the excitement-dampening information, Varsha got into the marriage, dreamy-eyed and hopeful. She was getting married after all!

Soon, she moved to the USA with her husband, leaving behind her job, her family and her dream of getting an MBA. She happily took on the responsibilities of a "bahu," learned to cook and changed her diet to suit what her husband needed to keep his sugar level in control. She dressed the way he liked, kept all the fasts, did all the recommended poojas to pray for his good health.

But the marriage slowly started turning into a nightmare despite Varsha's best efforts. Over the next two years, the dreamy, shy and quiet Varsha turned into a pragmatic, almost cynical woman. She endured abuse, betrayal and worse in this marriage. This passionate guy she thought she would eventually fall in love with soon turned abusive. This man she thought she could heal back to health with her love had an extra-marital affair all through their relationship. Lonely and isolated in a new country, she had no one to reach out to. She knew what her parents' reaction would be if she opened up to them about any of it, and so, she avoided doing that for the longest time.

It took Varsha many months to reconcile with the fact that this marriage could not be salvaged. The tag of a divorcee was unimaginable for her; she simply couldn't identify with it. She absolutely could not bear to disappoint her parents again. It took all the strength and courage that she could muster to get out of a relationship that she thought was forever. It was heart-breaking for her to realize that her life wasn't going to follow the path she dreamt of all her life. She wasn't going to get her happily-ever-after.

Once things got completely unbearable, Varsha filed for divorce. She fought a long-drawn and bitter divorce case alone without much support from her parents. And once that legal battle was over, she knew she couldn't stay back in India. How would her parents face their relatives and neighbours with a divorced daughter living with them? How would she bear with all the pity, taunts and unsolicited advice which she knew would come her way every day?

Varsha moved to Canada and started her life afresh. It wasn't easy in any way but it was somewhat liberating. It took her months to finally stop blaming herself or her parents. It took years to start building her new life, forgetting what had happened. Gradually, she made new friends, started painting and started a spiritual practice that grounded her and healed her. She picked up the broken pieces of her life and finally started living her life on her own terms. Last year, after studying for it for over 2 years, she got into one of the most prestigious MBA schools in the world. She gave up on the idea of a perfect soulmate years ago, but somehow, she never gave up on her dreams. And I have never been prouder of my friend!

#Prompt 5

1. If you are married or in a significant romantic relationship, let's write down things that your relationship brings to your life. Think of emotional value your partner brings – ways in which they might encourage you, ways in which they might be able to make you smile. Think of stability, think of love, think of companionship.

    Now, think of things you bring to the relationship. Be candid and don't underestimate the labour you bring to the table. Be mindful of creating an emotional balance and be aware of the value you bring to this pivotal relationship of your life.

2. If you are not yet married and see that you will be in your future, what do you want that relationship to look like? What are the things you would never compromise on? Before committing, travel with them and see what they like and dislike in food, places and people. Discuss religious beliefs and see how important it is for them. Know their views on family and parenting and the values that are important for them to be inculcated in children. Discuss their childhood traumas, happy memories and mental health. Discuss financial health; observe how they spend money and what they want to spend it on when they have more of it. See how they treat people who have less power than them. See how they treat other women in their lives – sister, mother, friend, ex-girlfriend. Discuss sexual expectations and fantasies. And most importantly, know that despite all the ticked boxes, "happily-ever-after" would need daily, continuous, mutual effort.

6

The Ideal *Bahu* Template

The one on marital bliss, traditions and identity crisis

"After these many years, if I didn't apply sindoor, it feels strange. I will look like a widow. A married woman should look like ghar ki Lakshmi."

"As a new bahu, I made the colossal mistake of asking my father-in-law, 'Aap pani lenge?' (Would you like some water?) Apparently, in my in-law's home, it was offensive to ask. We must simply offer water. I was schooled for days about many customs and riwaaz of this new place, many of which seemed rather irrational."

"My kids need to know that we are a family. If my husband and I have different names, that won't work, right?"

"As a bahu, I am supposed to engage with all the relatives we meet during weddings in the family or during pujas. I need to be interested in the rituals, dress up and play the part. My husband can be busy with his office work or simply be on his phone."

I have been called Amrita Purkayastha for more than two decades in this world. The first name is a bit too pedestrian, and if I were given an option, I would have picked a fancier name like Natasha, Shanaya or Afreen. My second name is a bit too long, way too difficult to pronounce or spell and has a patriarchal origin in the obvious sense that it is my father's family name. But by the time I could critically examine the pros and cons of my own name, it was late to argue with my driving license, passport, birth certificate and all the documents that proved I existed. As a coping mechanism, I used a fake Shanaya account on Yahoo chats till early 2005.

The single syllable noise of 'Ms' as a prefix to my name, making it Miss Amrita Purkayastha, was also acceptable, albeit grudgingly, when it was used in desperate airline announcements if I got late to board, or a professor used it when he found me giggling unnecessarily in class. My name, in various permutations and combinations, and various moods and tones, has been the specific phonetic stimulus I have responded to, to the best of my reflexes in this vast, cluttered and noisy world. It is what I have written on entrance exam forms, it is what made me blush when my crush said it out loud, it is what I have doodled during a boring lecture and it is what I scribbled once or twice on public property.

But since the big fest of mustard fish that was my wedding with Mr Aditya Shah, I have felt like the world has been looking at me with a glare that is somewhere between impatience and hostility. I simply cannot remain Ms Amrita Purkayastha and go on with my life, now that I have agreed to marry a bespectacled boy from the

Shah clan. There seems no good reason for me to be Mrs Purkayastha. I didn't marry Mr Purkayastha. I married Mr Shah. Simply put, I am too old for Miss and a bit too married for Ms. So, I must become Mrs Amrita Shah. If I don't comply, I am doomed to remain awkwardly miss-named (pun intended) and live in a fuzzy, confused realm where people would stare a bit too long at our ID proofs at hotels, where they will desperately look at me for other signs of marriage, where they will visibly wonder if Mr Shah and I have a stable, loving relationship.

'Miss' and 'Mrs' both have their origins in patriarchy. All these titles are derived from the word mistress. Miss meant a woman was yet to tie the knot, Mrs is to indicate that the pivotal life event has already taken place. Both prefixes were used as shorthand to indicate whether a woman belonged to her husband or her father. Via these prefixes, we basically ask women to give away a bit of their life to random strangers at electricity and gas companies, when men are not required to do anything similar. We expect women to change their names at a grown age to exhibit their marital status while no such thing even remotely exists for men.

In 2012, a crucial rule in the Family Courts Act was modified by Indian courts that made it legal for Indian women to retain their maiden name after marriage. Now, no law requires Indian women to change their names after they get married or after they get divorced. But driven by compulsion, convenience or choice, in most communities in India, and, in fact, the world over, women change their second names after they get married. It could be a surname or the husband's first name. In some Hindu caste groups in India, even the first names of women are changed based on auspicious numerology. So, while the law no longer dictates this, social conventions are clearly more powerful. It manifests as people demanding proof of marriage almost as proof of sincerity from married women. In several government offices and in public schools, paperwork is still unnecessarily cumbersome when the couple's surnames don't match.

Hidden in plain sight, in an innocent drop-down in online forms or in repeated questioning by government servants and neighbourhood aunties, in the twenty-first century, lies one of the most insidious assumptions that a woman's source of identity comes from the man in her life. The truth is, the surname changes and the prefixes are not merely tradition or some form of legal convenience. They are part of a system of markers that mark out married women from others. They are part of a culture that must know the man a woman is related to in order to decide whether or not she is worthy of respect.

The markers are not limited to the change in surname or prefix; married women are expected to change in terms of appearance as well. We can't simply agree to be in a committed relationship with a man; we need to demonstrate it very visibly. Every year, as I go home for Durga Puja, my mom looks at me with a disappointment greater than one she might have if I was caught in a drug scandal. Apparently, without my *sindoor, shakha pola* or *mangalsutra*, I look *obibahito* (unmarried), and what could be a greater shame for a married woman than to *look* unmarried. From *sindoor* to toe rings, from *mangalsutra* to *ghoonghat*, there is no escaping the symbols of marriage that only apply to women.

We have grown up watching Bollywood movies where *sindoor* is exalted to metaphysical levels. Heroines cry with happiness, their faces turned slightly upwards, shaking with part disbelief and part spiritual awakening when the hero fills their *maang* with the red powder, or in some cases, blood. While *sindoor's* relevance in contemporary Bollywood movies has become meme-ified with the iconic "*ek chutki sindoor*" parody in "Om Shanti Om," this symbol is not a thing of the past.

Interestingly, under the Goods and Services Tax rolled out in 2017, sindoor is tax exempted but menstrual hygiene products are in the 12% to 14% slab! The government clearly seems to know what the great Indian women cannot dispense with between the two. Modern, seemingly-liberated Bollywood actresses like Deepika Padukone or Anushka Sharma, who have broken all kinds of rules and glass ceilings, wore *sindoor* in their real-life designer-orchestrated Italian weddings. Globe-trotting, *Instagramming* Indian women have embraced these markers of marriage, albeit in their own styles. There is an almost gleeful embracing of these visible markers of patriarchy that previous generations of women were trying to avoid. Some wear their *choodhas* with designer bodycon gowns, others wear their mangalsutra over leather jackets. And the rest of us find an orgasmic euphoria in knowing that even while espousing modernity, our great Indian women of today have not forgotten their *sanskaars*. We feel comforted by the thought that the Indian married woman is still the epitome of *sanskaar* and *parampara*, the upholder of the sacrosanct, pure and unshakeable concept of *parivaar*. These dramatic words might have been erased from our daily vocabulary, but their essence is still very much part of our collective consciousness.

We might have forgotten why these symbols were put in place hundreds of years ago as essential symbols of a woman's chastity, love and fidelity towards her husband, but they continue to be an essential part of who we imagine being a good wife and a good woman. I am often told that my questioning of these traditional symbols for newly-wed women is much like those elitist, disdainful looks *'judgey'* people give to women who wear *salwar kameez* at a beach resort. They say, certain traditions might look out of place in the modern world, but that doesn't necessarily mean they are oppressive. I am told that many women who choose to take up these symbols of marriage wilfully now feel a reverse pressure to eschew everything that is traditional to seem progressive.

But traditions, however time-tested and precious, should be examined curiously for their relevance. Because for every young Bollywood actress who voluntarily chooses to wear the sindoor over her designer gown, there is still a young girl who is forced to adorn these badges of matrimony whether she wants to or not. For every woman who chooses to wear the *choodha* or the Mangalsutra as a style statement, there are a large number of women who are forced to give up on these when their husbands die. When these symbols of marriage are still so steeped in compulsion, rituals, force and rules, can the women who have a choice simply 'choose' for themselves without wondering what institutions are being unknowingly furthered? Can we pass these symbols on to our daughters in the future without knowing their history and their meanings?

These traditions that are taught as a badge of honour for good women are also deeply linked to the concept of family. In India, family is sacrosanct. We feel a sense of superiority about this innate part of our culture, looking at the western world's individualism with part disdain and part sympathy. There is a certain romanticism in the way we think of our families. These people are the warm, fuzzy blankets who promise to protect us from a cruel, indifferent world out there. They are the faces that stand next to us in precious photo albums, and these faces are part of our invaluable memories. It is almost impossible to define what family could mean for us. It could mean different things for different people, but for all of us, our family becomes a part of our identity. We carry a part of it with us wherever we are and wherever we go.

But while our family is an incredibly precious part of our lives, we find it difficult to objectively look at them or rationally judge their behaviour. We grow to believe that family is unquestionable and whatever comes along with it – the traditions, rules and restrictions – must be embraced. We are born in the custody of our families and grow up to be familiar with their flaws and idiosyncrasies.

Every family has its truth of homophobic parents, sexist uncles and caustic aunts. But we put up with them in the hope of love and future support. Almost like frequent flyer miles, we stay together to reap maximum benefits.

We go as far as to risk our emotional and mental well-being, knowingly or otherwise, for this imagined hope of security and comfort. And while everyone is supposed to come together to hold on to this beautiful concept of an ever-loving family, it is the women of the house on whom the responsibility of keeping this unit together befalls. It is on their adjustments, sacrifices and compromises that the harmony of the home stands firm.

Once married, the woman has a new family and she must forget those other people she had those precious memories and photo albums with. To keep her new *parivaar* together, an ideal *bahu* is expected to have some distinct mannerisms. She needs to be calm, respectful to elders, eager to help in the kitchen, tender towards all and fit in seamlessly. She is supposed to remember all the random extended family she is introduced to and get along with all of them instantly. When a neighbour comes knocking or an elderly gets sick, she is the one called on, while her husband remains distant and uninvolved. As a *bahu*, not having too many needs of her own and too strong opinions on anything are considered signs that she will have a *sukhi* family. The *auda* or *dulaar* (respect or affection) that comes to the new *bahu*, comes in exchange for the sacrifice of her individuality. The love, concern and care that the woman is promised in this new family of her in-laws, often comes at the expense of her autonomy and personhood.

According to Family Development Theory in Psychology, getting married is a major transitional stage of adult life that includes a variety of norms and roles. This influences the behaviour of new spouses, both the man and the woman, who take on the title of "husband" or "wife" and begin functioning according to social norms and structures attached to these new roles and begin integrating them into all facets of their lives. [11] This theory points to the possibility that often, the realities of the new roles do not fit with one's preconceived notions of themselves, pushing people toward a negotiation process called "identity bargaining." [12] Couples are known to have to work through boundary issues in the new relationship, their families and friendships, and they often struggle with adjusting to the demands and roles of marriage.[13]

As newly-wed women, when everyone around us is giggling and winking while taunting us about all the "marital bliss," we struggle to find some sense of congruence between who we thought we were and who we are now expected to be. The transition to marriage is a period of major psychological adjustment for women. The honeymoon period of the first couple of years, for most of us, is a paradoxical concept, as marriage causes severe emotional, cognitive, social, legal and economic upheaval in our lives.

For women, marriage becomes a time of incredible depersonalization which poses a solid challenge to personal identity. And yet, we spend no time acknowledging this. Absolutely no time is wasted in understanding the women's inner conflicts and struggles in her new home as a married woman. While we are still ravaged by the complexities of this new relationship, we scrape for ways to remind ourselves of who we truly are between the changes in our name, appearance and mannerism. All of this while worrying about our husband's meals or whether or not his shirts are ironed. We keep a smiling face while we wonder what made us the obvious candidate for kitchen and laundry responsibilities.

Women simply can't be themselves once they agree to get married. There are so many rules for women, so many "should dos" that as a survival tactic, women find ways to con the system. Some women wear long-sleeved *kurti* from home and change into trousers in their office washroom. Some have a secret kitty circle; others have a secret hobby. Some hide their whereabouts, others hide their opinions, likes and emotions. In many ways, small or big, we start living a dual life to make peace with ourselves and those around us.

In a constant battle between our identity and the ones we are supposed to love, we find ourselves in a state of dysphoria. We learn to make a million concessions for people around us, tip-toeing along a fine line to not ruffle any feathers and let the *sukh-shanti* of the home remain intact. But buried under layers of these compromises, sacrifices and lies, there creeps in a sense of inadequacy – a feeling of not being enough; not being worthy enough.

Women from across life contexts negotiate with the diktats of *sindoor*, name-change and the expected personality change when they get married. They espouse the virtues of a "good woman" and find their own small comfort zone within the restrictions and rules that apply. Depending on our specific environment, espousing these templates of ideal behaviours can give us acceptance, approval, love and in certain forms, power in our homes and communities. Subconsciously, we haggle with this system and partake in, what is called, a patriarchal bargain. [16] Sometimes, our decision to conform is a bargain, a strategic move that we unknowingly make to gain some control in our lives. And sometimes, it is because we take patriarchy as natural and inevitable.

Walking within boundaries gives us a sense of direction. It even makes us feel good about being virtuous. Disobedience, defiance or revolution are exhausting. Compliance is comforting. But the conformance to patriarchal traditions and behavioural templates that we think make our lives easy, chip away a part of our whole selves. The tricks we employ to keep everyone happy shrink our own self. In this process of negotiation, we unknowingly lose something precious. In this "*na teri na meri*" negotiation with patriarchal rules of marriage, we are left bereft of the most prized thing in this world – our true authentic selves.

Authenticity is when we live in accordance with our personal values, rather than according to the external demands of society in the form of conventions and duties. Multiple pieces of research in psychology have shown that authenticity is the bedrock of wellbeing. [14] Authenticity is strongly correlated with self-esteem, purpose, happiness and more. It is linked to psychological well-being, vitality, self-esteem and coping skills. Our ability to value our inner voice, to have congruence between our thoughts, emotions and actions is critical to living a happy life.

But a woman's authentic self is generally disposable in the construct of marriages. Our quest for authenticity could often be at loggerheads with our loving *parivaar*. But we must know that the promise of love that families make should first and foremost be showcased in being understood. It should be shown not in the obscure promise of future support, but in being treated with generosity and tenderness in the face of our flaws and real selves every day. Being loved shouldn't be so cumbersome. Being accepted shouldn't be conditional. Being able to voice our opinions and having a good relationship with our family shouldn't be an either-or option. There are ample places for opportunistic or manipulative relationships in this world and our homes shouldn't be such.

With one woman giving up on the *sindoor*, another one's life doesn't get easy. By one woman's insistence that she won't change her surname, another woman's family doesn't become more accepting. We are all living our own lives, with our own flawed but otherwise loving families, our own somewhat insecure but supportive partners and our own slightly nosey but helpful neighbours. We live in a world of contradictions and hypocrisies. We co-exist in a world of revolution and negotiation. And yet, it is undeniable that women's choices have a rub-off cumulative effect. In many ways, a woman who stands up for herself stands up for others around her.

For the sake of our own psychological congruence and not for some big societal change within our contexts, we must be able to make connections between personal choices and societal constructs. We must be able to question why is it that it is somehow more moral, more *Indian* to wear traditional symbols of marriage despite their oppressive origins? Why is it that as a society, we applaud women who conform to patriarchy with great harm done to their inner self?

Our personal choices are powerful in the context of our families and communities. Our conditioning might have taught us to value validation over our autonomy, but as grown women, we must be able to see the politics behind this. Despite the mental energy it takes to continually evaluate our values, options and actions, we must invest in it. Psychological congruence is an invaluable gift that we can give ourselves, and we must indulge in it.

Patriarchal traditions won't vanish overnight. We won't change the society we live in or our mental models in a blink with a single act of defiance. But in our little ways, with every act of defiance, we would find the courage to stand up for ourselves and who we are. We would find the courage within ourselves to be ok with garnering disfavour from others. We would possibly protect ourselves, albeit in a small way, from the crushing forces that disallow a married woman to have her own identity. We wouldn't then need to lie, pretend or hide.

#Prompt 6

List three marital roles in your life that you think are important to you: wife, daughter-in-law, sister-in-law, etc. Write just one word/phrase/sentence for each, not prioritized. Write what that relationship means to you and what it needs for you to make it work. It's best not to overthink. What rises to the surface as important now? Try and expand on those roles, writing about each of those aspects. Does performing any of these roles feel cumbersome? Which of these relationships do you feel nourish you and boost your inner wellbeing? Which of these feels like a lot of effort? Good or bad, our honest evaluation of our relationships empowers us to live them with more intent and presence. Also, think of identities and personalities you need to put on to make these relationships work. How do you need to modify or change yourself to fit into the expectations that come with them? What would the relationship look like if you were completely yourself?

7

"*Haq se Maango*": Sex, Intimacy and Compatibility

The one on feeling entitled to pleasure and more

Like most 90s kids, the song "*tip tip barsa pani*" from the movie *Mohra* was my earliest memory of anything distantly sexual. At that age, I liked watching the song and didn't exactly know why, and there was absolutely no way for me to find out. In my early adolescence, a friend from school introduced me to a porn site. In the age of big, bulky personal computers, I didn't have an option of accessing the site from an intimate, solitary setting. So, watching porn was almost like a top-secret espionage mission which was accompanied by both shame and excitement. I would carefully check if speakers were turned off, keep informative tabs open that could be toggled to just in case someone walked in, and after I was done, I would erase search history with the precision of a serial killer. While the idea of doing something sneaky was delightful, what I saw on screen was less than underwhelming.

My modem's screeching noise and the one made by the women in the scene seemed somewhat similar. The idea of romance with mystery and banter, something I had grown up reading in fairy tales and watched in Bollywood movies, seemed to have no place in this world. Sex in these clips was casual rather than intimate, and in many of them, the partners seemed to part ways without even exchanging names. Women in this world were dominated and disrespected. I wasn't just disappointed, I was heartbroken. By my 30s, when the novelty of sex had long weaned off, I realized that learning about sex and intimacy from porn was like taking driving lessons from the car chase sequences in Rohit Shetty's movies. Everything was unrealistic, exaggerated and nothing like real life.

Sex in the human world is complicated. It is loaded with judgement, shame, guilt, rules, power dynamics and more. Despite us desperately needing guidance on how to enjoy this universal experience and not struggle with a wide variety of emotional and psychological troubles that might come along with the experience of sex, it is almost banned from the vocabulary of young boys and girls. We speak in euphemisms whenever we want to talk about sex. From the two flowers snuggling or the bees kissing, there are a lot of layered, often incomprehensible symbolisms we use when we want to talk about sex. We simply aren't straight with it.

Young girls are shamed for even thinking about sex and young boys who want to know what to do and how to do it are shamed if they ask, since the assumption is that boys should already know. From formal textbooks and teachers, all you learn about is how the "thing" works. We see some unrecognizable diagram of things that we are told we have inside our bodies and we become vaguely aware of how babies are not flowers from God, but a Zygote of sperms and ova. There is absolutely nothing taught about consent and nothing even remotely mentioned about pleasure or orgasms.

Earlier, across many cultures of the world, there have been ways in which sex education was passed across generations. In Sierra Leone, women's secret societies passed on sexual knowledge and norms to adolescent girls. In Uganda, extended family members such as *ssenga* (paternal aunts) and *koja* (maternal uncles) did the same with boys and girls. The shunga culture in Japan had a liberated sexual discourse. They celebrated sexuality, often gifting explicit scrolls to newlywed daughters for the wedding night. Sex education was widespread, people explored their sexuality with confidence and pride.

Such institutions that taught about sex in a judgement-free, loving environment have weakened or disappeared altogether now. In our land of Kamasutra, sex was a natural part of family life and a way of enjoying one's body. It was an important lesson passed on to the younger generations. But our culture too embraced the British prudishness brought in by our colonial invaders in the 1800s.

There are a couple of goddess templates in Indian women's lives that tell us about the ideal template of feminine behaviour to which we must live up to. As little girls, we are supposed to be pious, pure and disciplined like Saraswati, the goddess of art and education. When we marry, we are supposed to transform into Laxmi, the goddess of wealth and prosperity, and become feminine, homely and dutiful. But post-marriage, when our lives start to become a bit colourful with the possibility of parents-approved sex, we somehow find no goddess template. The sinister omission of Rati, the goddess of seduction and desire, from the mainstream female goddesses, tells us about our culture's selective amnesia.

In our country, moral, good women are treated and represented as asexual beings. The ones that show even the slightest glimpse of desire are considered morally corrupt vamps. The worldview is stuck on using sex as a barometer to measure a woman's 'character.' Our *sanskaars* of purity and shame are reserved strictly for women, teaching them that bodily desire for us simply doesn't exist, and if it does, it absolutely shouldn't. We have lived with the binary all our lives – *sati* or sluts. We can only imagine women following these two templates. To even wonder, let alone talk, about our sexual pleasure is embarrassing if not shameful.

We teach young girls via movies, pop culture and more that we should wait for the man to approach us, to propose for marriage, to make the first move and initiate sex. In Bollywood movies, stalking and pestering are normalized by tens of blockbuster movies. Heterosexual romance largely showcases men in charge of initiating courtships. "*Hasseena Maan Jayegi,*" "*Hassi toh fassi,*" "*Uske Naa mein bhi haan hai*" are just creative ways of ignoring the woman's consent and often, outrightly violating it.

In the same universe, women are conditioned to expect to be chased and pursued and yet, be somewhat wary of this attention. What it really teaches women is that everything that happens in our love life is on the man's terms. We are but spectators, with no control or agency over when and how these things happen in our lives. Pleasure in a romantic interaction is a man's prerogative; we must simply play along coyishly.

Women are always someone being loved, someone who is a muse, someone with whom sex is had. They are always the objects and not the subjects who are equally participative in the two-person act. Accompanied by such an inert depiction of women's sexuality, there is often a narrative that men need it more than women do and that participating in sex is primarily for a man's desires. In many ways, we learn that men have some sort of uncontrollable sexual desire – driven by their physicality – that as women, we must understand and satisfy.

Unspeakable barbarity has happened in the name of men's sexual desires. Crass, impolite, discomforting sexual advances by men are condoned by "men will be men" tropes. There is a widespread benevolence for the ghastliest of acts by men and a widespread acceptance for some of the silliest acts. This comes from the understanding that male brains are somewhat differently wired; that men are more animalistic in their sexual needs and are often unable to control it.

But human brains are biologically and evolutionarily different from other animals. The development of the pre-frontal cortex in human brains, thousands of years ago, gave us the power to rise above our animalistic instincts.

It gave human brains the ability to absorb and rationalize all forms of inputs through conscious thought. There are infinite possibilities for a single input for our human brains. In no circumstance – even in extreme danger or hunger or even in the case of acute addiction – is our ability to think or decide for ourselves completely muted. It might be slightly compromised by instincts or habit or past experiences, but a sane human mind is simply not wired to be compelled by any input. The excuses the society then makes up for a man who violates a drunk woman, a skimpily clad woman or a woman out alone at night is patriarchy playing out and not biology. Because there is no biological compulsion to satisfy sexual arousal at the cost of harming another person. Men don't *need* to see women's naked bodies; they don't *need* to be sexually satisfied. They won't die if they don't get sex; it's not like oxygen. Let's not insult the poor, hard-working pre-frontal cortex of our brain by our "men will be men" tropes and accept that these are simple tricks to pardon entitled male behaviour fed by years of patriarchal culture.

In the parallel world of women, sexuality is only seen as important in the context of producing babies. A recent study in India claimed that roughly 70 per cent of Indian women do not orgasm every time they have sex. [17] Psychologists have found that many women in India do not experience orgasms ever. It seems if women had to orgasm to make babies, we could have easily controlled India's population!

Driven by shame about their bodies and sexuality, most women don't ever get a chance to explore what they enjoy in bed and only vaguely know what they dislike down there. Their orgasm is at best an unimportant detail in their lives and at worst, a shameful excess that they feel guilty about even thinking. Many women I met wondered if expressing their desires will make them look needy or wanting to experiment will make them less desirable to their partners who expect them to be shy and demure. Women learn that not only must they not express their sexual desires, but they must do all they can to protect the so-called "fragile male ego." Women focus on the man; faking orgasms is easier than telling the guy he has been doing things wrong. Women's satisfaction and pleasure have never been considered important, both by men and women, because sex has always been about what men wanted and needed.

To many in today's generation, it might seem odd that one can feel shame about their sexuality in today's day and age. Modern, enlightened women of the 21st century are supposed to be confident, enthusiastic and nonchalant about sex. And yet, many women struggle in those late-night escapades. Our complicated relationship with our sexuality is often not because of a simple ideological problem of looking at sex through a lens of a moral sin. It wasn't simply a political issue, although, in many ways, it might have been a major part of our conditioning and defined how we approach sex and intimacy as adults.

But being unable to express our desires of any kind is always much deeper than just ideology. It isn't something that can be dusted off with the reassuring sexual liberation of our generation. While the depiction and acceptance of sexually assertive women in our pop culture might have helped liberate us sexually, the feeling of shame about our sexuality – the awkwardness and guilt we feel about our impulses – is a deep-rooted psychological reality that needs psychological digging.

Emotional labour and intimacy need to be evaluated. A heterosexual marriage, for most people in India, is the first time they start living together with the opposite sex. Acclaimed research by Psychologist Dolan Miser highlighted how in most cultures people are ill-prepared to make marriages happy. In most societies, people are never explicitly trained in the skills that are helpful in maintaining love over a lifetime. Marriages need constant effort and most people are ill-equipped to handle such a pivotal adult relationship.

After elementary school, skills that help us form and sustain long-term bonds – listening, expressing gratitude, forgiveness, expression of love and patience – are rarely taught to us. We assume these abilities will come with maturity. And while women are somewhat naturally expected to learn the caring and nurturing abilities that are important for sustaining long-term relationships, we simply never teach men these values.

The emotional expectations from men in relationships are then laughably low. *Wow, he remembers your birthday! Umm*, I am his significant other, his companion in sickness and in health. *Wow! He babysits the kids!* The last I heard, it's still called parenting. *Wow! He helps you wash the dishes.* Well, he eats too!

We celebrate even basic decency when it comes to men. Women grow up believing that men come first. Their desires, pleasures and validation matter the most.

In romantic relationships, if women ever complain about the lack of emotional support or intimacy, someone or the other tells them how other men are worse. We placate ourselves thinking that we are fortunate to have a man who does the bare minimum. That seems more than enough.

What if we didn't have such low standards for men in our lives. What if we expected partnership and compatibility and not just basic decency from them? What if we reinvented the idea of sex as a mutual exchange of trust and pleasure, where it is not only about mutual consent but also about mutual pleasure? As women, we must know that we have as much agency in the act and our pleasure is as important. What would our lives and relationships look like if we felt entitled to sexual and emotional effort from our partners?

For millennial women like me, it might have taken many years of being in a loving, stable relationship to understand what worked for them. Contradictory signals from the pop culture we grew up around must have confused us and thrown us off in different directions in our journey of realizing our sexual needs. I know that it took me many years of fighting inner monologues to be unabashed about desiring and expressing what I liked and disliked not just in the bedroom but in my relationship. What forms of affection felt suffocating, what kind of gestures made me swoon and what kind of intimacy felt right. And it all started with me feeling entitled to it. It all started with me stopping myself from ignoring my discomfort. For younger women who have grown up in the world of high-speed internet, anonymous browsing and women's communities, this journey could be smoother as they can learn from older women's experiences. Much like equal pay, access to education and a world devoid of discrimination, pleasure, intimacy and emotional labour in a relationship are women's *haqq* and it is time that we claim it!

#Prompt 7

What is on your mind and in your heart that you find hard to express in real life to your partner? What did they do physically that hurt you or made you uncomfortable that you couldn't articulate it even to yourself? Not just sexually, but emotional and psychological satisfaction is important in romantic relationships. Have you been comfortable feeling entitled to your desires and wants?

You may find that expressing it on the page is useful preparation for expressing it in real life. But there is no hurry to do that. Let's fight our demons within our minds first. Start by identifying what is it that you want – sexually and emotionally – in your relationships. You also may find it useful to write as a private exercise to work out your thoughts and feelings on your own to interact with your partner more productively in general.

Here is an example of a letter shared by a woman that could help you think better for yourself…

Dear partner,

I need solitary time in the bathroom without worrying about the noises I am making and whether or not you can hear the flush. I love necking and foreplay and that shouldn't be a dispensable activity on the bed. Make the effort; notice my reactions and moans. Yes, every single time.

I am responsible for my own actions and well-being, but every now and then, you would need to mend my broken heart when I can't do so myself. I promise to smother your broken heart with love whenever needed. In case your family and I are in a me vs. them kind of situation, you would give me a patient hearing. Much like the glorious *"chaand pe daag,"* I too can have flaws and insecurities and they sometimes might manifest in awkward, weird situations. All I want for you is to have kindness and patience. That's really all one needs in relationships. Bear with my moods, flaws and warts, because I am so much more than that.

Are you ready to write a letter on your own?

Motherhood

8

To Birth or Not to Birth

"My mother-in-law has started keeping jagrata, vrats, pujas back home for us to have a baby. I am 31 years old and the pressure is unbearable. She is well-meaning and I love her. But isn't this manipulative?"

"Having a baby changed my life for the better. Here, see his pictures; he is adorable!"

"We didn't want the second child. We simply weren't ready financially. But I couldn't bear the thought of abortion. It was my own choice; I wasn't forced by anyone."

"I had an abortion when I conceived for the second time. It was the worst timing; I didn't have a job then and we had just shifted to a new country. I didn't tell anyone and got the procedure done secretly. After 5 years, I don't think a lot about it. Maybe, I should feel regret?"

"I won't be loved, respected or accepted in my husband's family if I tell them I don't want to have a baby. Both of us don't want kids and we are thinking of concocting a medical problem. At least then, they would let us both be."

"It is not as if I don't have maternal instincts, or I am not a responsible person. In fact, I grew up taking care of my younger brother and three little next-door neighbours who were no less than brothers to me. I almost consider my brother as my first born. After him, I had my nephew and niece to shower with my love. With them around, I have never really felt that I am missing anything really. Also, my father was diagnosed with Parkinson's disease when my brother was still pursuing his degree. So, I had to make myself available within a few hours' notice whenever an emergency arose. And that happened multiple times. I could not have done that if I had children to look after. Eventually, with time, the decision to not have children just became obvious to us."

Every time I breach the topic of choice of motherhood and discuss the pros and cons of becoming a biological mother, I am shushed, sometimes rather vehemently. Any attempt to objectively evaluate this universally accepted feminine role is simply discarded and is often followed by audible sounds of *"haye haye"* and *"tsch tsch."* I am solemnly told, with a make-believe patience one conjures when one sees a child wrapped in his own poop, that I would understand what it means to be a mother when I *become* a mother. I would understand selfless love when I *become* a mother. I would understand the boundless joy and unbridled meaning when I *become* a mother. That an average woman might try and think for herself whether or not to have children remains one of the most disturbing thoughts for many, much like that kid and his poop.

Being a 34-year-old married woman myself makes this discussion unintentionally personal, despite my abundant attempts at keeping this research-based. I simply want this decision to be data-backed. Before my engineering admission, I spent months searching the internet, speaking to friends, random uncles and neighbours to decide on my specialization. Before buying a TV, I had comparative prices from 4 different sites and reviews from at least 3 friends. I have 30+ items in my shopping cart on Myntra at any given time, and if that has taught me one thing, it is to do nothing if you are undecided.

But for how long? I should have had my baby's sonogram polaroid to fan the candles on my 30th birthday, right? Time is running short on making this decision, I am told. At my age, it might already be too late for me. The great "biological clock" is ticking, and I must decide now, lest everything around me implodes.

Thankfully, research says the biological clock is a well-struck metaphor from the 1970s and is not a neutral fact about women's bodies. The history of the term "biological clock" is also the history of mixing science with sexism. It is a true example of how assumptions about gender shape scientific research and how discoveries are often used, possibly unintentionally, to serve sexist goals. [18] Recent studies have corroborated that the difference in pregnancy rates at age 28 and 37 is only about 4 percentage points. [19]

Fertility does decrease with age, but the decline is not at all steep enough to keep women in their 30s to lose sleep. The ubiquitous "baby panic" that women must have children by the age of 30 or at best early thirties is based largely on questionable data. Multiple recent studies support having children until 40; many environmentalists highly recommend waiting till 35 for your first child and completely rejecting the idea of a second. The biological clock then is essentially a psychological manipulation. We should be comforted with the knowledge that there is no need to panic and there isn't a ticking bomb in our ovaries. Let's not allow alarmist relatives and nosey neighbours to push us into being a parent before we are ready.

But even if I have been able to '*shush*' the biological clock's ticking for now, how can I know how it will go for me, not the pregnancy but the motherhood? Would I find the joy people have promised that comes with children? Or would I find misery that I have often seen with my own eyes? I am at the cusp of being either elevated to a god-like pedestal if I choose to put my ovaries to good use in the next couple of years, or risk being the vamp in the lives of everyone I know and is somehow seen to be personally attacking everything that families stand for.

Howsoever I wish the female body came with an in-built noise cancellation feature, it doesn't. When my friends, who showed no pre-disposition of wanting kids till a couple of years back, suddenly become mothers and can't stop gushing about their baby or when my parents, for whom I have lived all my life trying to impress, show disappointment at me for not planning my kid's 5th birthday already, my resolve tumbles and my research feels pointless. Have I been fooling myself by thinking that I have a real choice in the matter? I've often wondered, do women really have a choice on whether they want to embrace motherhood? Or are we so effectively socialised into the role almost since our own childhood that we don't recognise that we *can* choose to opt-out? If autonomy is a quintessential human good, why do women have little or no choice in the matter of motherhood? *Haye Haye*!

There are many reasons for wanting to become a parent. Once the biological or evolutionary argument was put to rest, which, by the way, comes mostly from middle-aged men on Whatsapp, I got to the emotional reasons. There were many emotional motherhood stories I encountered in my interviews.

Nancy Jose, 42 years old, from Bangalore, spoke about it passionately. Her story stood out because nothing about Nancy seemed conventional – a relatively late marriage which was out of her religion and a career graph which moved from being a chef to becoming a lawyer. She seemed to defy traditional set paths all her life. When she gave birth to twins, she quit her job, which I imagined must have been an incredibly difficult choice to make. But she said that those initial years were the most beautiful years of her life. She could breastfeed her twin boys, be a part of every little firsts – to simply be a mother and nothing else.

Her voice was full of emotions and the honesty was unmistakable. She recollected many stories from those years which made me go '*aww*' multiple times during the conversation. I could sense the sheer joy when she talked about her boys.

Another woman, Noopur, 48 years old, spoke descriptively about the moment she held her newborn daughter in her hands almost 20 years back. She said she still remembers how overwhelmed she felt with the sense of responsibility and love. She said she felt like she had a ball of clay in her hands and it was for her to make a human being out of it.

Love makes our world go around. I can imagine the passionate love one must feel for an actual human being that you have created, nurtured and pushed out of your own body. Loving another human being is an incredibly beautiful thing. Mothers I met and spoke to showed me a window into what unwavering, all-encompassing love could look like. Being able to nurture or nourish another living being is a profound experience. Many of us feel that quintessential 'maternal' instinct for somebody in our lives. It could be an elderly parent for some, a pet or a spouse for others. Someone we can walk through fire for.

We all know that being loved is magical, but I have also come to realize that being able to love someone else deeply is equally magnificent. Love is a remarkable warm, fuzzy feeling that makes us better people. Loving someone unlocks something divine within us. It truly does. It can bring immense meaning and fulfilment. To care for another person, to live for someone's happiness is a crazy, irrational thing that modern research is starting to measure as a huge determinant of our wellbeing.

Every human being wants to pursue something bigger than who they are. There is a constant want to be part of something purposeful. And I have heard many stories to conclude that motherhood does bring that elusive feeling of meaning, even if momentarily while the kids are quietly sleeping. That feeling that one's life is significant or purposeful may even be necessary for human psychological functioning.

But what we mistakenly assume is that this precious sense of purpose can be found in a singular way for women. It can, in fact, be found in different places by different people. Some find it in their art, some in their careers and some in their children. This glorious, purposeful journey of parenting is often not prescribed with as much coaxing to men. If men announce that they never want kids, they get a pat on the back and there's a joking 'lucky, you dodged the bullet!' But if a woman dares to find her sense of purpose in anything other than nurturing another human, there are constant 'oh, you immature thing, I can't believe you're missing out on the most beautiful experience. You must be so sad and lonely.' That's when this glorious, fulfilling love becomes gendered.

There is an implicit contempt in the insistence that women's lives can be fulfilled only with motherhood. It tells women that their lives are not worth living on their own; that it needs to depend on somebody else and that it needs to take on an identity based on somebody else to be complete. Similar labels of relationships – father, son, husband – are not as implicitly branded to a man's identity or masculinity. But motherhood is the ultimate testament of one's femininity and a male child is the ultimate achievement of female life.

We define women's lives by their relationships, something we don't seem to be so eager to do for men. For women, being a mother becomes somewhat of a personality trait. Once a woman becomes a mother, we think of her more softly, judge her more considerately and we even respect her more. The idea of all women wanting children is so deeply ingrained in our collective consciousness that we do not understand the women who choose not to. We look at them with suspicion. They are perceived as a threat. This is a widespread, culturally-inculcated cognitive bias.

It is important to evaluate and do the requisite psychological digging on the choice of motherhood. Behavioural theorist B. F. Skinner postulated it in one of the most fundamental theories about psychology called operant conditioning – the consequences of actions (ours and others) influence our future involuntary behaviour. We not only watch what people do, but we also watch what happens when they do what they do. We are more likely to imitate behaviour that is rewarded and refrain from behaviour that is punished.

Women internalize the social standing of childless women; they observe the disdain for women who do not have kids either voluntarily or due to medical conditions. Childfree women are tagged as selfish, immature, characterless or pitiful. The ones with children are considered more compassionate, respectable and virtuous. With such deeply held biases, the choice of motherhood often becomes involuntary or instinctive and is not a well-formed choice.

We don't stop and check for ourselves what brings us joy – what is it that we truly want to do with our limited time on the planet? Do we want children because we want to be admired as the respectable sort of woman?

Or because we want to be the perfect kind of woman, a woman with not just a career, but also an ability to nurture? Or do we want to show the world that we have a body that can make babies and we have someone who wants to make babies with us? Over the years, under the influence of our partners, parents, families, religion, doctors and others, we struggle to make a decision that is truly meaningful to us.

While we would imagine women worldwide must be spending a good part of their 20s and 30s trying to arrive at a decision if or why they want to be a mother, statistics say that the choice is often made for them by *becoming* pregnant before *planning* for it. An analysis of 33 studies of fertility intentions in developed countries found that roughly one-fifth to one-third of women who become pregnant aren't sure whether they actually want a baby. Research says, nearly half the pregnancies worldwide are unplanned. Not necessarily unwanted, simply unplanned. Just pause for a second and think about it. Think about those millions of women around the world, every year, who find themselves bearing a child, inside their bodies, they simply didn't plan for. Even if millions of conceptions are unplanned, there are millions of such pregnancies that are taken to term.

Roughly 40% of unplanned pregnancies are terminated by abortion, globally. [20] Women's right to decide 'when and if' they want to be mothers is fundamental to how we experience our lives and sexuality. But in many countries of the world, abortion is still looked at as a reckless idea, much like drunken driving. Motherhood should be of choice and willingness. To be a mother without one's choice is akin to being a slave. And to imagine that in certain counties this choice still doesn't lie with the woman legally is barbaric and unimaginable.

Being implicit in the assumption that a foetus has human rights is the belief that women don't. Do you know why we allow religion, morality, culture, etc., to govern women's bodies? It's simply because the world is run by the "inseminators" and not the "bearers." The moral and cultural codes of our world are made by men, thinking of men. Quick trivia –Viagra, the pill that helps men get an erection, was invented before the epidural, the medicine which is used to lessen pain during childbirth. Many countries approved sales of Viagra several years before they approved any modern forms of birth control. Our history tells us in different ways that we as a civilization value a man's bodily pleasure over a woman's bodily autonomy.

Statistics say abortion rates are similar across countries with lenient and strict abortion laws. In countries with strict abortion laws, the rate of abortions isn't low; they are simply far more dangerous. But it is not tough to gather that despite abortion being legal in India, it is still a tremendous taboo. Even amongst progressive, urban, working-class women. I have met many women who described one or more of their kids as unplanned and mistimed. Unless the woman was actively planning the conception, preparing herself physically and mentally for a lifelong commitment, why does she feel compelled to carry through? Women said they didn't choose to abort due to a variety of reasons ranging from "what if we are unable to conceive later" to "what if I regret it later" and the extreme "abortion is murder."

There is so much uncertainty, misinformation and fear around abortion, and yet, we have so little material to go by. While aunts, mothers and neighbours openly talk about conception and pregnancy, they never breach the topic of abortion. It is a shame that women can't share it even with their closest ones. It's often done completely alone, with at best a partner or a close friend in the know. I'm not suggesting we post about our abortions on Instagram or scream it from the rooftops, but it's still an issue with significant opposition, both legal and cultural. But a de-stigmatization of abortion and more conversation around it could make the choice of motherhood more informed for millions of women. It is estimated that 15.6 million abortions take place in India every year. [21] If such a large quantum of men were going through something common, there would be widespread articles, panel discussions and mass rallies about it.

Motherhood is often touted as the ultimate testament of one's femininity and the sacrosanct goal of a woman's life. As women get closer to their 30s and have a socially accepted partner of the opposite sex, they are suddenly, often magically, expected to develop a nurturing streak and grow a deep natural desire to reproduce. The ambitious woman who was chasing career milestones for most of her adult life is now suddenly supposed to re-calibrate her life goals and find a mate if not found already and create a new human being, lest her biological clock stops ticking.

But a life-long role of being a mother must be a choice borne out of unwavering willingness and absolute clarity. It should be scrutinized and double-guessed with at least a year-long rigorous self-analysis. Ink-tests, psycho-analysis, all types of personality tests and at least 3 different types of "10 signs you want to be a mother" tests. Unless you are literally fantasizing about Taimur-Ali-Khan instead of Shahrukh Khan, you should keep the pill and use protection. No amount of "*haye/haye*" should stop you from making a well-informed decision about something that would fundamentally change your body, lifestyle, relationships and every part of your life.

We must remember that a child is not something to have, but something to do. The doing is what seemed hard; the having always seems marvellous. It is also not a single-person job. All mothers rightly deserve a lifetime of unquestioned gratitude for forty painful weeks of lodging and boarding, many hours of labour and several months of breastfeeding. But the pedestalization of motherhood shouldn't free fathers to be distant observers.

At the risk of giving credence to the child-less, unhinged, prototype Feminists are always pictured as I might be one of *those* feminists. The one people sympathize with for missing out on life, the one people don't call for their kids' birthday party. Even if I have found myself spending an embarrassing amount of time looking at Taimur Ali Khan and marvelling at his almost edible cuteness, I don't feel like I am missing any meaning in my child-free life. Aditya and I are so sure of this at this point that our sex life is probably more cautious and calculated than our financial investments. I have two different apps which tell me my least fertile window and he uses protection with unmatched discipline. We have never experienced a better example of our glorious teamwork and understanding.

We are told by everyone around us that we are immature. We are made to feel as if we have not settled yet. But we wholeheartedly reject the holy trinity of marriage, homeownership and parenthood as the testament to being an adult. We vote, pay taxes and have a clean home. That is as much adulting we can agree to do. Too bad that I was born with the ability to reproduce; I don't wish to use it. Thanks for the ovaries, it's bad enough I must deal with its monthly tantrums and pointless melodrama. I don't wish to use them any more than I absolutely must. Not at the moment anyway.

Unfortunately, I know that one of the intrinsic features of the human condition is that there is no such thing as a cost-free choice. Making choices are 100% easier than living them. We spend so much of our lives obsessing over making the right choices for ourselves – so many books, blogs and more are dedicated to helping us make the big decisions of our lives – what type of career we should choose, the kind of partner we should marry, whether or not have kids, whether or not to have that haircut, etc. Instead, we should really be investing our time in developing tools to be able to live with our choices.

There is no such thing as the "right" choice. It is unfortunate that most parents are too awkward to admit this, but no honest evaluation of parenting experience is complete without accepting that in some ways, children could be both the meaning of one's life and the cause of deep misery. All choices bring in their own joy, struggles, learnings and regret. I know I will regret it if I stick to my current choice and birth control plan. I know that I will regret it if I change my mind in the future. Before I decide to have kids, I am trying to understand as much as possible about Aditya and my specific taste in misery – what kind of sacrifices are we ready to make, what sort of regrets are we ready to bear with. Because both choices – being a parent or not – will involve specific discontents for both of us along this hopefully long life we'll live together.

Given that I am the bearer of the ovaries and the dairy-producing glands, the decision will have a higher impact on me. And I must know that there is nothing glorious about embracing motherhood and there isn't anything shameful about being child-free. Both of us will be, at many points, very unhappy with whatever we eventually choose. We will be tired, sore, irritable and guilty with kids around and we will be lonely, desperate and confused without them. With either option, our teamwork and understanding as a couple will be tested brutally. With either option, I am more likely than him to feel alone. I am likely to be judged more harshly than he ever will be. This is why there is just one thing I am sure of at the moment as an ambivalent 30-something-year-old married woman – I commit to being open and honest about my experience to myself and to others near me. I will be open about my regrets, pains and fears. Motherhood is one of the most difficult projects that I might undertake. It might be one of the biggest lost opportunities of my life.

9

"Maa Toh Maa Hoti Hai" – The Pedestalization That Hurts

"I had dengue once and had to be hospitalized. Those were the only 4 days that I slept well in over 4 years as my kids were taken care of by my husband. Those were the only 4 days I was being taken care of. It felt blissful."

"How many cups of pretend tea can one drink enthusiastically in the span of an hour! I am exhausted by this game with my daughter! I need some adult conversations and connections."

"Everyone seems to be a better mother than me."

"When I am with my daughters, and I am with them a lot, I feel like myself but a little muted. I can't actually hear many of my own desires or needs because their desires and needs scream so loud. Which is fine. They're still so young. I know it's temporary."

◡

I grew up in the home of a perfect mother. Ma was always dutiful, adjusting and perfect. Her home was always tidy, her kids were well-mannered, and she made three-course dinner every day. She managed all of this while holding a travel-intensive government job. She was my alarm clock, my moral compass, my ride and my teacher. Now, after many years, as I look back, I am somewhat heartbroken to realize that as a kid, I didn't fully see her. It feels like I *couldn't* fully see her; I was too close, too blinded by my own needs.

Who was Ma when not with me? Was there any version of hers that was not my mother? As a kid, I remember seeing little brown spots on Ma's hands, where drops of hot oil had sputtered out when she fried fish. Why did I assume she felt no pain? When we came home after a long day, Ma went straight to the kitchen to make us dinner. Why did I assume she didn't feel tired like the rest of us? Why didn't we feel a sense of complete awe towards our super-human, ever-loving Ma? Why did we take her affection, attention and space for granted? Why did we feel entitled to all her sacrifices? And most importantly, why did she never teach us to be like her?

We spent most of our time with Ma, but she mostly talked of the heroic and fun stuff Baba did. There was something intrinsically disadvantaged in her role in the house that didn't inspire an ambition in me to follow her path. She was perfect herself, but she always allowed us to feel entitled, to be flawed – easily forgiven, pampered and indulged – something nobody seemed to extend to her. I now know that of all her incalculable gifts of kindness in my life, this has probably been the biggest of all.

Much like an entitled kid, our society too claims that there is something we don't entirely understand about perfect, godly mothers of the world. Something almost divine and other-worldly. We call it a "natural part of motherhood" or "nature's blessing." We claim to not understand her – how does she simply *know* what her child wants? Where does her super-human strength come from? We imagine there is something metaphysical, something that gets hard-wired into the female body while giving birth. *Miracle of life! Ah, the wonders of being a mother!*

As a society, we live comfortably in our warm, fuzzy imagination and lack understanding of all the sacrifices and selflessness our mothers deeply reward us with. We look away from the possibility that mothers can be human. We stop ourselves from thinking she might be in pain, confusion or despair because her all-bearing divinity feels so much more comfortable. We skillfully craft this invisible idealistic role which is played not by a goddess but by a very real woman in flesh and blood because it allows *us* to continue to be flawed.

Ma – is not a word, not even a simple role. It is a whole mood. It is the biggest supporting role in the drama of human life. We have glorified this in many ways – from religious texts to the most clichéd movies. From *"mere paas ma hai"* to *"ma toh ma hoti hai."* From Mother India to Mother Nature. With such iconography and their repeated occurrence, we consistently impose a set of qualities that are to be universally considered determinants of maternal identity. Mothers become symbols of our culture and become part of our rose-tinted imagination. There seems to be a universal template of motherhood – something everybody seems to instinctively know: self-sacrificing, selfless, pure and free of desires.

There is something deeply sinister in this. We must concede that patriarchy is clever and sly. The glorified template of motherhood is one of patriarchy's signature moves and it is one *hell* of a move! Idolising motherhood is a blatant misogynist justification that is wrapped neatly in "good intentions" for extracting disproportionate emotional and physical labour from women. The perceived glorification expects women to sacrifice their time, ambition and a sense of self for the higher purpose of motherhood, which is supposedly way more worthy than their own individual identity.

This glorification doesn't bring higher respect for women. That's a rookie mistake to confuse pedestalization with empowerment. Despite all the warm fuzzy feelings, it's the father who is the *head* of the family. It's his name the child writes on his passport. It is his family to which the child belongs. Instead, the pedestalization of motherhood is to render women unreachable. It ultimately leads to the isolation of mothers from the world of humans.

Women are so conditioned to this perfect mother prototype that we feel happier with praise and compliments about our maternal feats than to openly acknowledge how incredibly tough it is. Having grown up in this world of glorified mothers, women find it terribly hard to ask for help. It is flabbergasting how much we think that we are simply expected to know about how to raise children. Mothers are just supposed to know, we are told. But mothers are not a homogenous segment of people.

Some have the temperament to deal with the baby right on the very first day, some take months to do so.

Some have easy pregnancies, some not so much. The ones who breastfeed worry they are doing it wrong or doing it for too long; the ones who can't breastfeed feel helpless. The ones who don't feel automatically connected to the child feel evil; the ones who do aren't sure if they are right. Working mothers feel guilty and the stay-at-home ones feel judged. Moms desperately search the internet for the "best baby food," "the best way to burp the baby," "best diaper for summers," and along with the answers, they find a million ways they are doing mommy-hood *wrong*. Every mother feels guilty and imagines they are ruining their children's lives despite trying their absolute best. Every other mother seems like doing a better job, being a better mother. Every mother second-guesses her choices even if motherhood is the single most demanding role she has ever undertaken.

By constantly showing how effortless maternal love is and how easy it is for mothers to do so much, we tell the ones struggling that they are failing. Women end up taking on disproportionate burdens alone that they should ideally share with their husbands because she doesn't trust him to do the task perfectly and, god forbid, anything is less than perfect with the kids! If the world would have spent any time normalizing the variety of experiences women have as mothers, most of them won't feel so desperately out of breath. They won't feel like they've signed up for something much more overwhelming than they ever thought was possible.

According to research done by WHO in 2017, 1 in 5 women in India experience post-partum depression. That's 20% of women, and these are simply reported numbers.

Like any other mental health issue, the real numbers must be much more. What triggers postpartum depression, or PPD, can vary widely. It could range from worrying if the baby is eating too much or too less, to lack of emotional and/or financial support, distressed relationships and even domestic violence. Too many cases of PPD go unreported because the focus shifts entirely from the mother to the baby after delivery. The mother's well-being is no longer as important once a healthy baby is delivered. The whole family which obsessed over the mother's health during the months of pregnancy finds no time to notice it now. Make no mistake, I did meet many happy, beaming mothers through my research. But then, there were mothers who were exhausted, unfulfilled and deeply lonely – something they couldn't quite say, but it was palpably real. In such debilitating noise of loud constant sermons about how mothers should be it seemed like these women had lost the connection with their own humanity.

But despite the evident drawbacks, women all over the world are voluntarily signing up for motherhood. What is it then that keeps mothers going? And most of them seem rather happy with their decision. Most mothers I met said that some days did end up in tears of exhaustion, but they insisted that tears didn't outweigh the joy. Even on the worst day, they felt an incomprehensible connection to their children – a love so deep they felt their hearts would explode. They also felt deeply fulfilled and committed to their children.

Psychologically, is there something gratifying about living up to our ideals? For example, the deep and passionate patriotism that the soldiers give up their lives for is often incomprehensible to the rest of us. Many soldiers across the world fight for their country in a quest for oil, land or independence from western occupation. Soldiers on both ends of the field feel like they are fighting for the larger cause, a greater good. To many looking at them from a distance, they seem brainwashed. The arbitrary idea of nationhood and fighting for it might seem like a big political conspiracy. But for those on the field, it is everything. For those fighting, it is their calling, their life's mission.

The causes we are convinced are worthy of our sacrifice become larger than us. When we are convinced that we are doing things for a bigger cause – that there is no better goal, no higher purpose than what we are committed to – human beings can go to any extent. If we can imagine such profound love for an arbitrary notion of a country or a football team, it shouldn't be surprising to see women sacrificing their all for their kids. This thing we call parental love has biological, neurological and psychological origins.

From insects to primates, researchers have been able to connect the link between dopamine-receptor genes and behavioural interactions between parents and their kids. Humans and other mammals have a highly evolved system that motivates them to care for their children. Simply put, parents are *genetically* coded to find joy and happiness through a dopamine reward system when they spend time with their offspring. Parents, not simply mothers. Children with pudgy little toes and fingers are incredibly cute and smell great. Their touch and smell physically activate the centres of our brains that give us a sense of joy. Kids somehow reset the clock for their parents and extract a kind, giving side that the parents had probably disconnected from before they became parents.

Giving our all to someone or any form of self-sacrifice for love could be deeply rewarding. There is something deeply satisfying in altruism that selfishness can never bring us. The benefits of giving to our psychological health extend across the life span. Research confirms, for example, that college students who provided social support to their roommates report decreased symptoms of depression and anxiety. High school students who offered to help strangers report a more positive mood. Even toddlers with no understanding of societal rewards of altruistic behaviour benefit from giving to others — showing greater happiness when giving their treats to others compared with those who just received treats themselves.

These, among many other findings, suggest that in our everyday life, giving is beneficial for us. It has been associated with positive psychological health, good physical health or decreased mortality, and improved relationships. It also distracts us from our own problems, enhances meaning in life, increases self-efficacy and feelings of competence and improves mood. Caring for someone and being 'giving' in our relationships – not just for those who are the creation of our ovaries – has been proven to be a great way to improve our psychological health.

Instead of being shushed into believing the glorified template of motherhood and dispelling our efforts of understanding mothers, we must understand the patently human motivation for it and the psychological rewards that could come with it for many of us. We must forget the metaphysical level we imagine mothers graduate into overnight after giving birth. We must know that mothers too are humans and operate very much within the psychological and emotional realm of regular human beings.

We give selflessly because it brings us fulfilment. We love because it activates a side in us that feels great. And while we do so, we must forget the loaded dialogues and the flawless templates and begin to see it for what it is – parenthood. A gender-agnostic relationship of caregiving. A deeply rewarding relationship with another human being. An incredibly difficult and highly impactful role for society. And most importantly, something that should be equally prescribed to men. Since selfless love is so emotionally rewarding, we must teach men the trick.

By reframing motherhood as a choice, a responsibility a woman can willingly take on, for the possibly selfish reason of finding fulfilment in their lives, we will shift the power back to the women. By refusing the dubious accolades of martyrdom that motherhood is supposed to bring, by rejecting the unachievable standards of perfection, mothers can connect back to their humanity and know the joys that parenting can bring. They would know what real physical joy spending time with our children can bring. Raising a family is hard work, but it could also be one of the most meaningful tasks of our lives. If only we can look beyond the *dialoguebaazi.*

#A Little Bit of Nudge

I wish my ma, *mashis* and *pishis* were taught a little more self-love and a little less self-sacrifice. Self-love isn't the same thing as being selfish. I understand life-long relationships do not survive without giving and unconditional affection, more so for the relationship with kids who basically are an investment (emotional, physical and financial) for over two decades. But I wish our mothers and aunts could value themselves a little more. Their hunger, emotions, pain, sleep and fatigue should matter, at least in their own eyes.

We have all grown up with a few selfless, sacrificial women in our life or known someone who fits that template. Someone who simply puts her needs on a back-burner day in and day out. Instead of participating in and gaining from her pedestalization, can we find small ways of nudging her to do things for herself?

#Prompt 8: For Mothers

Below is a writing prompt designed by Dr Martha Beck, a sociologist and life coach, who has spent more than 20 years teaching women how to break free from society's pressures.

To fully understand how a self-sacrificial maternal template is impacting your life, keep a running journal of specific situations in which you've gone to unreasonable lengths to make life easy for your kids or partner. If your efforts were acknowledged, make note of how long any feelings of appreciation lasted and the mood and emotions you felt then. Keep track of how you felt about yourself after the event and any changes in your behaviour towards your family.

Make a separate list for instances in which you make a point, not to self-sacrifice and keep track of your thoughts and feelings along with your family's response.

Beauty

*The one on body image,
shame and self-worth*

10

Beauty = Love: The Power and Currency of Being Pretty

The one about beauty, desirability, and self-love

"In our MBA campus, this was common knowledge – only pretty girls got shortlisted for certain companies and roles."

"If you are a pretty girl, your life becomes easy. I was not one of those girls; I was studious and hard-working. Boys only spoke to me when they needed my notes. They had their power; I had mine!"

For many years, as a teenage girl, I imagined a relationship with the (then popular) cricketer Ajay Jadeja. In moments of secret roleplays with friends, I used to call him '*mere woh*.' I had vivid dreams of the day I would go to watch him play, he would see me on the big screen in the stadium and instantly fall in love with me. In some versions of this passionate love affair, I also win the Miss India beauty pageant as Mr Jadeja falls hopelessly in love with me while on the judge's panel.

In all these versions of my future that seemed equally realistic at the time, the onus of being 'fallen in love with' was entirely on my imagined earth-shattering beauty. In the present, however, I was a dark-skinned, chubby girl with an average nose, wide shoulders and unremarkable eyes. But there was an outrageous fantasy I harboured that these traits would vanish when I grow up. If I slathered enough curd and *besan* or used the right shampoo, surely God would take care of the rest? And once he does the needful, I didn't have to do much more than just a shy smile here and a coy blush there. I wanted to grow up and be beautiful because I didn't have to be much else if I was that. I just needed to be effortlessly pretty and innocently unaware of it.

I don't remember what prompted these imaginations in the 13-year-old me. Looking back, I realize I was fed this through many stories, movies and anecdotes. The fairy tales I read, talked descriptively about women's beauty and romanticised the template of love at first sight. There was always an average girl and a powerful man. So many movies had shown me a similar pattern. When I met more women, many narrated a somewhat similar childhood dream involving some form of a beauty pageant, some form of love at first sight and a charming powerful man. To most of us, it appeared as this almost obvious and non-negotiable truth of the world that for us girls, beauty = love.

Not simply romantic love; we believed that being valued in any way in this world depended entirely on us being beautiful. I had this rather unshakeable belief that I won't be loved, heard or treasured if my skin darkens, if my gums show too much while laughing or if my waist isn't a certain inch. It took me half a lifetime to unlearn that problematic model of love. It took me many years to realize that I am entitled to lose flesh and gummy laughs and still be 100% worthy of love.

The brain, among its many other functions, is a beauty detector. Even when not doing so consciously, brains are quick to determine attractiveness. In its hurry to judge and get cognitive closure – a trait it has learnt as a survival tactic – our brains become prone to cognitive bias or judgment discrepancy when it comes to people's appearance. This gives those who are traditionally beautiful a widely researched and universally accepted unfair advantage in this world. An example of the "halo effect" that human minds are vulnerable to is the attractiveness stereotype.

Research has proven that we tend to involuntarily assign positive qualities and traits to physically attractive people. [22] We judge them to have higher morality, better mental health and greater intelligence. [22] In simpler words, the human mind's laziness or propensity to simplify the incredibly complex world in which we live makes beauty a powerful currency to get a lot of things in this world – power, acceptance, free lunches, lenient punishment, undeserved attention and much more. A mix of youth, attractiveness and desirability guarantees acceptance, attention and adoration. It also promises influence and power. Be it talking an officer out of a traffic ticket or walking in without a reservation and getting a table at a restaurant or talking that co-worker into helping you move some furniture – being considered pretty is a solid, undeniable advantage.

Women learn this not-so-secret power of beauty through many years of conditioning. In a world run by men, since the days of Cleopatra and Helen of Troy, physical attractiveness, has possibly been the only real currency women had. Whether to be noticed, to be heard, to be taken seriously or to earn millions selling products, being beautiful is one asset women know they can leverage at any time – one true power they could yield. Little girls are encouraged to exploit her cuteness. She is not directly taught how to do this, but she picks this up from experience. During adolescence, girls learn that their appearance is the best resource to get attention and validation. Use that power and flaunt it! Bat your eyes and get the class notes. Smile and get out of punishment.

One would think how amazing it must be to be a young, attractive girl in this world, isn't it? But the big open secret is that world over, adolescent girls face extreme body image issues. Research in India (a country considered rather conservative in terms of extreme beauty ideals) showed over 77% of girls had deep body image issues. [23] Let me repeat that, 77% of Indian adolescent girls. Multiple pieces of research have corroborated that feelings of self-worth are strongly related to feelings of physical attractiveness, and globally, on average, roughly 44% of adolescent girls and 23% of adolescent boys downright 'feel ugly and unattractive.' [24]

Low body image has been deeply linked to depression, eating disorders and dysfunctional relationships. Possibly unintentional, but a ruthless mechanism of objectification and peer pressure works in our social groups, families and neighbourhoods to make us feel ugly. We learn incredible nastiness towards the ugly ones and yet, most researchers point out that most of us feel ugly on most days. Ironically enough, the power we are often told that comes with an enchanting, pretty smile, just doesn't bring us enough reasons to smile.

Since beauty is so powerful and ugliness so belittling, it is worth exploring what exactly becomes beautiful for us. India has had a history of white-skinned invaders who became the ruling class and the oppressed *Bahujans* and Dalits who were persistently coerced into outdoor manual labour. It created a deep cultural association between dark skin and 'low' social status – a correlation that refuses to take its leave much after the white rulers left. A simple dearth of melanin somehow became a token of power, status and eventually, beauty and desirability. Europeanness has been the universal touchstone of desirability and appeal. In terms of beauty standards, Eurocentricity is the monstrous phenomenon that made the princesses in even our desi fairy tales blue-eyed and fair-skinned and the brown-skinned characters that actually looked more like the real us were the princess's ugly sisters. This is a pervasive, prehistoric pandemic that we are yet to find a vaccination for.

There are social, historical, cultural and evolutionary drivers of what gets defined as physical beauty ideals in human societies. We, individual humans, are not the sculptors of our bodies and we are not the ones who get to design our inner workings. We aren't the ones who can calibrate the hormones or the melanin. When it comes to our own bodies, there is a lot that we don't seem to have any control over. If we are being honest, being considered beautiful without the make-up and the butt-lift is validation for something that isn't entirely attributable to us. And despite that, we let this define us. We worry about this validation all the time.

Some of us do win the lottery of the perfect anglicised nose but worry about our bunny teeth. Some of us are blessed with great metabolism but worry about our frizzy hair. There is this constant chase for perfection which nobody in the world seems to be able to achieve. This glorious beauty, which most of us don't seem to have at the moment, promises us attention from people with questionable judgement and makes us imagine rewards that we don't really deserve. One can't really *see* oneself all the time. So, aspiring for beauty is simply aspiring for constant external validation. It is about externalizing the source of one's self-worth. This pursuit of beauty-power, therefore, becomes a no-win game. Linking how we look to how we feel is a way of linking our well-being to something we have minimal agency on. It is like going all-in in a roulette game for our emotional wellness. And we all play that risky game all our lives.

While all gender identities struggle with body image issues in this unkind, hyper-visual culture, it is still deeply gendered. We all have heard Smriti Irani's weight being used to attack her on prime-time television, Mayawati and Mamata Banerjee's appearances are made into memes and constantly made fun of while Amit Shah's bald head or paunch goes undissected. The world reserves its most judgemental, impolite and unempathetic side for women in the public eye. It seems to stem from the fact that many men are still incredibly unused to seeing women as anything other than "beauties" and, therefore, must reduce them to their bodies to make sense of their identity. They can only relate to women as wives or mothers, or just a piece of flesh to admire or shame. They admire Hema Malini's smooth cheeks and shame Renuka Chowdhary's excess weight to deflect from the cognitive dissonance their brains experience as a woman becomes their equal or becomes successful. A woman's choice of attire, hairstyle or use of make-up is closely watched to judge her personality and character. To be taken seriously, women must conform to the guidelines on feminine behaviour and beauty standards constantly.

And such continuous scrutiny of their own bodies or the ones of women in the public eye makes us self-conscious and unsure. As we feel constantly evaluated for what we wear and how we look, we end up spending a disproportionate number of hours and money directly or indirectly on looking our best.

Women narrated anecdotes of how for a family function, they start planning their saree weeks in advance, while their husbands pick up something at the last hour. It is an outcome of systemic and continuous subliminal messaging to women that how we look would be evaluated and that would define us. I have personally seen women who have barged through the hierarchies of the workforce, broken all sorts of a glass ceiling and even got their partners to fold laundry secretly retouching their make-up before a panel discussion while their male counterparts are reading their notes.

But the funny thing is that the scrutiny about her appearance that constantly follows a woman doesn't stop with her treading the line. As we spend all our lives trying to live up to the beauty ideas, we are also made to double guess. We are told any interest in beauty is frivolous and vain. Skincare and make-up are often deemed dumb, claiming that women of opinion and substance cannot like make-up or high heels. We have two neat boxes beauty-without-intelligence or intelligence-without-beauty. We are allowed a mind or a body but not both. We mock cosmetics and self-care even while telling women to be naturally perfect. We *are* supposed to look beautiful but without working too hard for it. We are supposed to be sexy but not too much as to be known slutty. We are supposed to be voluptuous, not fat, thin but not flat. Books are for some; beauty is for others.

One can only have this or that, but not too much either way. And so, women are constantly balancing over a thin and delicate line of what is beautiful and what is moral, what is frivolous and what is substantive, living in a constant state of insecurity and doubt. And this is the most insidious impact of the beauty power on women's psychology. We are never really sure of ourselves. We start looking at ourselves through other people's eyes. We know that if we don't fit society's standards of desirability, we won't be worthy of anything, and yet, if we care too much, we will never be taken seriously.

This has an unquantifiable impact on our lives and personalities. We miss the moments, the conversations and the experiences. We are constantly watching ourselves, correcting our smile, hiding our fat as well as our concealer, double guessing our hairstyle as well as our intelligence, and amidst all of this, we experience life a little less and *live* a little less. What could possibly be more oppressive?

All through those years of imagining a love at first sight saga with Ajay Jadeja, I desperately tried to live up to the ideals of beauty. Perhaps, I was desperate to prove something, or perhaps, I had been made, repeatedly, to think that. A huge chunk of my self-worth was dedicated to approval from the boys in my life. Their opinion about me seemed to matter as much as, if not more than, my own. It was much before it was a practical reality that I doodled the name of my prince charming in my notebooks. I was desperate for some dude, however unworthy himself, to think I'm so perfect. It isn't easy to shake off that glorious idea of love as we meet the real world of judgements, taunts and unkind comments. As I developed the desire to be desired, my body started belonging a bit less to me. Instead, it belonged to the world outside; it belonged to an imaginary notion of love at first sight that was not just impractical, but if it turned into reality, would have been seriously toxic.

I didn't know it then, but implicit in my desire for drastic changes in my body was self-loathing. It was as if I believed that the way he saw me would change the way I saw myself. That model of love that I dreamt of was based on self-hatred. How paradoxical! I often wonder, when did that start? Where did I learn that? What did that gaze that diminished me look like in my own eyes for the first time? Was it that neighbour who called me "*sawli*" (dark) and recommended a tube of fairness cream or was it that bully who told me my lips were too big?

It took many years of introspection, reading and knowing the world and possibly, some stable, loving relationships to realize that I didn't owe the world the effort to look pretty. That my body is my private property and its upkeep is my personal business. I started looking at this gawky, unloved body of mine with empathy. For the first time, I realized that it was, in fact, fucking amazing – this much-hated body of mine. It can do a far greater number of *Kapalbhati* rounds than many can imagine. It can bend in ways which surprise even me. And more than anything, this unloved, abused body is the only one I got.

At the end of it all, 'accepting and loving oneself' is truly the answer, however cliché'd it may sound. There is no substitute for being 'Ok' with yourself. But as an over-thinking, introspective, self-help book consuming 30-year-old, I have come to know that it is a mission that takes a lifetime of learning, forgetting, crying-in-bed and relearning all over again. Accepting us for who we are doesn't come naturally most of the days. It needs continuous and deliberate work. And yet, it is the only thing that is worth working on all our lives.

Beauty, it turns out, is not just something to behold and consume but something to create and do in our lives. That power that we imagine comes with beauty – confidence, self-assured sexuality, individuality and identity – has nothing to do with how we look but everything to do with who we are. And that is the only power we have in this world – the power to build ourselves, to re-build ourselves when we fall, to help build this world into something better, to hustle, to dream, to be whimsical and silly and to do all of this without needing a nod of validation from others.

Crests and Troughs – My Beauty Journey

By Sankhya Samhita, Singapore

***

The first time I looked at myself in the mirror and wondered if I was pretty was at the age of 18. Born into a very academic family, I was taught from a very young age that how you look is the least important thing about you. I sailed through the otherwise turbulent teenage years without once stopping to think if I was fat or thin. All I knew was that I loved to play dress-up with Ma's sarees and an almost empty tube of lipstick a cousin had once left behind, hoping I would throw it away for her. Ma didn't wear any make-up at all because my father firmly believed that a woman should flaunt only her natural beauty. Everything else was superfluous.

At 18, I went out of my hometown to pursue my Bachelor's degree and stayed at a hostel. The first month was extremely difficult for me. In addition to being homesick, I hated the food. I skipped meals, never intentionally, but because I couldn't bring myself to eat. By the time I went back home a month later, I had lost a ton of weight. And everybody who saw me commented on how much prettier I looked now that I had lost weight – a weight I never knew I needed to lose.

Just like that, a switch somewhere inside me was turned on. For the first time in my life, people noticed me for how

I looked. For the first time in my life, it occurred to me that I could be pretty too. As easily as that, the association was made – thinner is prettier.

Once I went back to my hostel, I started intentionally skipping meals. It didn't help that the guy I was dating during that time was reed-thin. The more I paid attention to what people had to say about the way I looked, the less I looked within myself. How I felt during the day was determined by how much food I had eaten that day. If I skipped most of my meals, I'd feel accomplished and proud. If I caved in and had food, I'd feel guilty and promise to myself that the next day would be better. The thinner I got, the more attractive I thought I became.

And that, dear readers, was the beginning of the slippery slope that landed me in full-blown anorexia, except of course, during that time, I wasn't informed enough to recognise it for what it was – a serious eating disorder.

Having completed my graduation, I came back home to pursue my master's from a University based in my hometown. Being close to home suddenly made things a little better. Breaking up from that toxic relationship helped further. I was eating marginally better, but I still wasn't feeling at home in my own body. I remember taking a walk around the campus one day when a friend who knew me from before commented on how I had put on weight. I was still thin, he was quick to note, but I used to be thinner, he added. That one comment sent me spiralling down for weeks after. The association had been made and it was tough to break.

Three years later, I got married and moved to Vietnam. Away from everyone who knew me, it felt like a fresh start.

I was a delirious newly-wed, drunk on love and a sense of adventure, and while I still attached a lot of self-worth to how I looked, it somehow didn't matter as much. Romantic dinners to celebrate each milestone month, fragrant hotpots that warmed my belly and soul, pizzas to celebrate mid-week and butter chicken to celebrate Fridays at the only north-Indian restaurant in Hanoi, I wouldn't trade those experiences for anything.

We welcomed our daughter two years after we got married and I became the delirious mother of a very clingy baby. I also became visibly fatter, something that everyone in my vicinity took no time to point out each time they met me. Because I was breastfeeding exclusively, I had a very limited wardrobe to choose from, and because I would breastfeed her all the time, my clothes would anyway be crumpled. Because I had no time to go out, my eyebrows were out of shape, and because I didn't have time to work out, so was my body. Until one day, I realised that I didn't want to look in the mirror because I didn't like what I saw. I had turned into my worst nightmare. I stopped caring how I looked, stopped caring how I dressed because none of it seemed to matter. My wardrobe consisted of loose t-shirts and baggy shorts, especially because I would only go out to run errands. I felt dejected, but at the same time, not motivated enough to do anything about it.

And then, one lazy afternoon, clearing out my drawers while trying to entertain my two-year-old, I stumbled upon a red lipstick — one from my wedding. Something inside me ached, thinking about that young bride with stars in her eyes. Without thinking why, I put on that red lipstick. The shade was quite aptly called 'Bridal Shower.' I looked in the mirror, and for the first time in a long time, I smiled.

I was still the same woman, nothing had really changed and yet... and yet, my reflection was someone different. I promised myself I would never let myself slip again. I promised never to be dressed like a slob again, even if it was to go to the supermarket. I started buying dressy stuff again. That red lipstick reminded me of who I could be. Each time I wore my red lipstick, I felt like I could conquer the world.

Over the course of the next few years, I stumbled upon the concept of body neutrality – the idea that while you might not really like your body on all days, you accept it for what it is and realise that you are so much more than how you look. Perhaps, because of the way I was raised as a child, this felt like a homecoming. I started intentionally tuning out intrusive thoughts about my body, choosing instead to focus on loving myself for who I am.

It's been a long and arduous journey, but I think I am finally in a place where I can look at myself in the mirror and see not fat arms, but arms that carried my girls (my younger is now a year old). I don't see my obviously bulgy belly; I see a womb that nurtured two healthy babies. I don't see wrinkles around my eyes; I see lines from laughing. I am grateful for everything my body has done for me and I respect its needs instead of subjecting it to deprivation. I have my good days when I love the way I look, and on bad days (yes, it's perfectly natural to have them as well) there's always my red lipstick to make me feel good!

#Prompt 9

Write some of your own endearing quirks – non-physical stuff that makes you irresistible. Things you do that bring incredible joy to those around you. Things that make you entitled to love, respect and adoration. Your sense of humour that can light up the most boring conversations and your ability to know when to use it. Your ability to see who is hurting and who is struggling and find the exact right words to pull them up. Maybe, it is your ability to think of a solution on your feet when everyone around you is losing their shit. Think of all those wonderful things that make you worthy of all the great things in life that have nothing to do with how amazing you could look in skinny jeans.

Be specific, try and imagine in as much detail as possible. Don't feel shy; this is a simple exercise in giving ourselves a compliment. When was the last time you did that?

Connect with others with similar stories on @everyday.revolution_ on Instagram.

11

Beauty Regimes, Billboards and the Conundrum of Choice

"Bikini wax hurts but what choice do we have? I feel so unclean without doing it."

"I want skin like Anushka Sharma. Flawless. It glows even without make-up. I have tried so many products, but these acne marks simply don't go."

"I bought two bikinis for my honeymoon and I have never since had the body to wear them. I know they say every body is a bikini body, but come-on! I would look so ugly in them today!"

"I am eagerly waiting to be a 70-year-old with saggy boobs and wrinkles and finally not having to obsess over my body. It must be liberating, no?"

I stopped threading my eyebrows a few years back. In June 2017, I had dengue for a month and I missed going to the parlour to shape my rather scanty eyebrows. As I recovered, instead of wanting to go out, meet friends and eat all the fries in the world, all I could think of was getting an appointment at the salon. It might have been the papaya leaf from my dengue prescription, but I realized I needed to stop these compulsive monthly visits. I was fatigued by years of constant gaze by my well-intentioned stylists – being told that tying my hair made my face look big or being recommended a de-tan facial, even when I had not spent a day out in the sun. I was simply done.

I started seeing the insidious ways capitalistic consumerism and patriarchal beauty standards worked together in convincing us to voluntarily undergo these unnecessary and painful procedures. Having never undergone labour pain and with *mata-rani-ki-kripa* having painless periods, threading and waxing were the biggest traumas my female-born body had to endure as an adult. To be honest, I have minimal and invisible hair growth in most places on my body. So, this didn't really feel like a big bold revolution at the time. It helped that my hairy underarms saved me thousands of rupees on an annualized basis, but it is still slightly embarrassing to have learnt such a big life lesson because of a mosquito.

To be honest, it wasn't just a daytime mosquito that changed my beauty regime forever. It was, in fact, many years of introspection and double guessing. When it comes to beauty rituals, make-up or clothing, I have never really been entirely comfortable with my choices. If painful hair removal was NOT OK, why did I still buy painful stilettos? And if heels were bad, weren't wired-bras worse? If I rolled my eyes and obsessively tweeted about the air-brushed beauty ideals propagated by magazines and movies, why did I still have two full pouches of make-up and more than necessary pairs of earrings? Was it simply hypocrisy or was it years of internalized patriarchy, or were all of these simply my expression of femininity that needed to be left alone? Red lipstick, mascara or high heels, to wear them or not to wear them, what they mean or don't mean have been a point of focus for many of my diary pages and peer debates. Every time I put on my favourite lipstick and pout, I often paused and reflected on why exactly am I doing this. After a couple of minutes of deep reflection, as I remembered the WhatsApp forward propagated stereotype of how women take forever to get ready, I sigh and give up.

My love for make-up started very early. At the age of 4, I put my mother's sindoor on my lips to ape the bright red lipstick I saw on television. This love for kohl eyes and red lips was the only reason I agreed to take up *Bharatnatyam* dance lessons at the age of 7. For my textbook typical Bengali parents, it was either that or Hindustani Music, one of which involved me playing the un-glamorous Harmonium. But being in a dance class meant I had make-up. During stage performances, it was fun to see my face transform with lipstick. The eyeliner seemed nothing less than magic. Make-up was fun and something I could choose to pick up entirely voluntarily, albeit within my dance classes. At school, it was shunned and penalized, and as a "good girl," I grew up with a healthy disregard for "those girls" who sneaked lipstick into the class.

As an adult woman, make-up almost seems like a necessity. Cosmetics and costly make-up products feed into an obsessive culture of consumerism. In today's world, even teenage girls are expected to be dressed and dolled up daily. Women are peddled products, rituals, surgeries and diets *constantly*. We are also taught very specific beauty rules – 'no horizontal stripes if you are broad,' 'if you have fat arms, then no sleeveless,' 'no midis if you are short.'

Implicit in every beauty rule is a special category of insecurity. We are conditioned to waste years scrutinizing, doubting and ultimately, hating parts, if not all of ourselves, based entirely on "problems" that can be solved only by buying products from an industry that invented these problems in the first place. We are fed a constant discontent about how we look and then, offered a discount on a product that would change that feeling. Rather convenient, isn't it? We are told that to be happy, all we need is a solid foundation – not of kindness or self-belief, but the other type that could even our skin tone. And when all is said and done, what is the prize for this self-torture? Fitting neatly into the destructive narrative of female beauty.

The consumerist world has craftily made us believe that high heels and make-up have the power to transform not just women's looks, but also their mood and level of self-confidence! Women are told that they should wear heels not to simply look taller but to feel more feminine and sharper. These are a part of our performance of femininity. My sensible, comfortable shoes were unfeminine, and feminine shoes didn't seem very sensible.

Feminine apparel has been senseless for a very long time. In not-so-distant history, women used to wear corsets that were laced so tightly that their breathing was restricted and led to faintness. They used to compress the abdominal organs, which led to poor digestion and caused atrophy in back muscles. Even today, we have women's pants designed to be so tight that they don't have the space to accommodate pockets. We have cropped sweatshirts that leave the waist bare in winter. World over, the norms of feminine beauty and fashion are driven by the male gaze. It is precisely why we have clothing trends that sexualize the female body. It is the male fetish for long legs, deep cleavage and slim waist that defines women's clothing and results in the creation of tight skirts, high heels and cropped tops.

In service of the male gaze, images of women in media are almost always perfect and sexualized. The magic of *Adobe Photoshop* is that a simple click can smoothen the skin and a mouse drag can lift eyebrows and sculpt the jawline. And today, even that isn't needed, we have Instagram filters to do that for us instantly. Everything can be made thin in seconds – neck, thighs, arms. We are constantly served a system-created ideal of completely unachievable beauty day in and day out.

Selling products to women based on this narrow template has grown to terribly disproportionate heights in this suffocating capitalistic world. The pervasive reach of these images via television, magazines, billboards and now, social media means that this fake ideal is transmitted on a far larger scale than ever before. From creams to insensible shoes, women are used as cogs in this structure and fed products created by those who think of women as faceless, homogeneous entities who don't know what they want unless packaged in glossy covers.

In South Korea today, one in five women has had cosmetic surgery done. In Brazil, even young working-class women regularly invest in tummy tucks and the country's signature butt lift. Deeply ingrained insecurities are instilled and fed by newer trends and ideals every single day. We are exposed repeatedly to a world of manufactured beauty that is nothing less than relentless psychological warfare. As we encounter these artificially created images of female beauty that are highly uncommon and largely unattainable, our brains struggle with 'upward social comparison' and experience discontent, depression, anxiety and more.

Research suggests that product advertisements can convey meaning that is beyond the physical characteristics and consumers grasp implicit meaning through associations and cultural knowledge. [25] Scholars have suggested that products provide certain insights about their buyers and that this extended self means products become part of a consumer's self-concept. Any marketeer worth their *Excel* sheets know that advertisements are supposed to make lifeless objects emotionally relevant to their buyers. Advertisers spend millions of dollars across the world to research and understand their consumer's most intimate, vulnerable needs. And with that data, they craft creatives that make consumers relate the advertisement to themselves. For example, the meaning of a high-heeled shoe in an advertisement is different from the meaning of the same shoe conveyed outside of its advertisement context. Outside of advertising, the shoe is a relatively distant, neutral product, but in an advertising creative, the shoe becomes a desirable product that suggests an attractive self-image on buying it. Merely placing a product in an advertisement can transform it into a self-relevant product, which, in turn, causes dramatic changes in the effects these products have on their consumers.

Such faulty advertisement is exactly how Beauty becomes the Beast in our lives. In 2004, research done by The School of Psychology at Flinders University of South Australia concluded that exposure to advertisements instantly increased negative mood and body dissatisfaction amongst women. Even short exposure to thin-ideal female images led to negative moods and body dissatisfaction, which disturbed the researchers because their study contained far fewer images than a typical magazine. There have been several other studies that have definitively been able to link consumption of fashion magazines, television and movies with body dissatisfaction in women. [26]

In 2006, a study in Basic and Applied Social Psychology for Washington University concluded that we underestimate the negative effects of advertisement by relying primarily on measures of explicit body image. [27] Although people may be able to maintain positive self-views at a conscious and explicit level, they may be less able to do so on an unconscious and implicit level. These air-brushed images in advertisements that we are exposed to for years are not fully understood to be an unattainable feat that we can rationally reject. They form within us a pang of unconscious guilt. Without articulating it in these many words, even in our own heads, somehow, we feel we owe it to the world to look pretty. This becomes a lifelong pursuit. We don't seek answers to questions like *do I really need what I am buying?* We feel dirty if we don't painfully remove every strand of hair from our bodies. We forget to treat ourselves with kindness as we continue the relentless chase to look like those people on the billboards.

According to the consumer-culture impact model created in 2008 by Helga Dittmar, our culture is characterized by two dominant ideals: the "body-perfect ideal" and the "material good life ideal." The "body-perfect ideal" refers to all the beauty ideas – ultra-thin, white skin, big eyes, etc., for women and ultra-muscular, tall-built for men. The "material good life ideal" refers to affluence and a luxurious lifestyle. The model postulated that over generations, these two cultural ideals have become deeply linked because they are constantly shown together in the media. Movies, advertisements and art perpetuate the notion that one achieves both – ideal attractive looks and lavish lifestyles – together.

In the Indian context, given that class is deeply linked with caste, the body-perfect ideal becomes deeply linked with the high-caste ideal. It strengthens the association of usual beauty templates like white skin, tall build, sharp nose or thick moustache with brahmin/upper caste. Big noses aren't ugly, curly hair isn't unkempt and dark complexion isn't dirty, but it is our brain that is deeply conditioned to euro-centric beauty ideals via movies, art, advertising, etc.

It is the duty of poets, painters, novelists, designers and television producers to help us live good lives. And since most don't take it as their duty to do better, we as consumers must choose better. It is important we guard ourselves against the harmful ways advertisements manipulate us. We must consciously be able to look beyond the beautiful, glossy promises made in the adverts and see the consumerist world for what it is.

Advertising or movies or pop music could be art that is used for good. What matters, is we, as consumers, carefully choose the things we admire. Who do we look up to? What do we consider beautiful and why? Good-looking celebrities can deeply influence our outlook, our ideas and our conduct. And bad heroes give glamour to flaws of character and misguide us into believing stalking is cool or that violence in slow motion is beautiful. We must find ways of stepping away from this world of airbrushed models and photoshopped images and look at it for what it is.

As I struggled to reconcile my love for make-up with Feminism, I gathered that Feminism itself cannot be against the act of make-up or a type of skirt nor is it against the act of letting *parlour-wali didi* remove the last microscopic blackhead from our nose that is somehow visible only to her. It couldn't be against a cosmetic or fitness regime or a fashion choice, for that matter. This movement was started on the ground of following women's choices and not accepting a set of arbitrary rules set by others. But choice, as a concept, acquires a new meaning when we live amidst subtle, insidious and constant manipulation every day.

Manipulation is a complicated and deliberate process. We need to look into our individual choices when it appears that for us to have self-confidence, we need to have a concealer. When we believe we need big boobs to be desirable, we need to stop and ponder. When we have bad hair days that turn into bad-mood days, that is when we need active questioning. This manipulation happens via carefully choreographed celebrity weddings, it happens via orchestrated airport looks and candid pictures. Remember, manipulation occurs through consent and not coercion anymore.

It is not going to be simple. Just because we learn to see the world more rationally, it doesn't mean we can easily untie ourselves from years of conditioning. We have learnt through many years and millions of signals, not just through advertisements, to hate what we think is ugly. We have learnt to zoom in on our body's imperfections and see them as personal failures. This brutality towards others and more importantly to our own selves will be difficult to unlearn. But we must try constantly.

I love make-up-loving, clothes-obsessed, heels-wearing women. Hell, I am one of them on most days. Anything from a place of joy and comfort shouldn't be questioned. Individual choices must be looked at with benevolence rather than judgements. For ourselves and for women around us. If high-heeled footwear makes you feel strong and smart, you do you. And if you feel like it doesn't, there is no cause for you to feel frumpy or inadequate in your flat canvas shoes.

When it becomes more about our flaws and less about our well-being, we should protect ourselves against this consumerist world that cons us into believing we need a product to be happy or we need the right clothes to be confident. We don't. To paraphrase what *Yogis* have been saying for thousands of years, all human experience comes from within. We might play this world's silly games – wear heels to that meeting, wear lipstick to win over our crush, get that *Botox* to extend our showbiz career by a couple of years. But we cannot, ABSOLUTELY cannot, link our inner well-being to any of these.

And in that context, our choices of feminine expression should be evaluated by us; our projection of femininity should be dissected by us. Not by others in the form of judgements but evaluated and understood by ourselves with curiosity and empathy. Our choices, when made from a place of awareness, could liberate us. We might conform, but that acquiescence won't come from our disadvantaged place. Are we making a conscious choice or are we socialized to conform? Can we do both within the same week? Yes, we can. On some days, we might need to stop being an activist and just crack that difficult sales pitch in high heels. But on other days, we must stand back and see how and why high heels have become so deeply linked with our confidence. Sometimes, with red lipstick or even a body-shaper that flattens our tummy, we have one less mental battle to fight for the day. But on other days, we might want to look deeper into our mental models of aesthetics, fat-phobia and femininity.

First, we need slow and gradual unblinding to see these patterns. The interconnectedness of patriarchy, consumeristic economy and unachievable beauty ideas. We must be able to step back and see the politics in our personal choices. We must be able to question our own choices and look deeper into their origins. I agree; not every bit of personal style needs to carry a political statement, but we can still fight our battles under our receding hypocrisy while making small bold progress in our lives. We might love shopping, clothes, anklets, heels, lipstick, fake eyelashes or body-shapers, but our self-worth shouldn't be dependent on any of these.

It would take creating new mental models and topping them up with new information for us to undo years of manipulation. The new mental model will be cognitive reasoning – knowing how beauty ideals are not absolute and are simply a form of *dhoka* that keeps changing forms every couple of years. It is to know how Kardashian sisters are deeply troubled and the gravity-defying butts and logic-defying lips peddled by them is a problematic business model. We must make efforts to delink our confidence, happiness and self-worth with looking beautiful. How we present ourselves to the world is a form of self-expression – a conscious choice that we should make from a place of joy. If it is being made from a place of shame, fear or guilt, it's time we reject that.

Knowing we have a choice will free us up. While individuals unlearn, society needs to do better. We need new information, new signals and new stimuli of influencers who are body positive, of people who are kind and loving. The ability to love oneself is a learned trait and we need to surround ourselves with the voices of self-love and not just the noises of insecurities. When we wear make-up as a form of self-expression, experiment with it, play with it, instead of living up to some arbitrary trend. When we get off the treadmill of endless products, fad diets and painful procedures and take a walk in the garden of acceptance and self-love, that's when we will truly know beauty. Because beauty was never a thing to be; it was always a thing to do.

#Prompt 10

Write about some of the amazing stuff your body can do. Remember that the things that are awesome are not just the ones you have but also, the problems you don't have. Please don't feel ashamed of sounding conceited or self-obsessed. In a world that tells you constantly to feel ugly and inadequate, showing oneself some love is an act of revolution. We do need a brash, loud voice in our head, possibly with a misplaced confidence of a roadside catcaller, to tell us we are beautiful, to counter those subtle, overt, consistent voices that told us otherwise.

Go ahead and show yourself some love. Write shamelessly about all the wonderful things your body has and the things it could do.

Examples:

I have an amazing smile. I don't have to worry about my gums, my teeth or my lips. Because my smile reaches my eyes and they twinkle. It lights up my whole body and it feels fabulous!

I have a very flexible body. Any dance move, any yoga position, with some practice and patience, I can do with precision.

12

Dear Body-Shamers – F*ck You!

The one about objectification, shame and healing

"My thin cousin said she would rather die than be fat like me. Is fat really the worst thing a human being can be? Is fat worse than being vindictive, jealous, shallow, cruel or boring? When I was 13 years old, it felt like it was."

"Sahil was the best-looking guy in the batch, which meant he could get away with a lot. Not just with girls but also with professors and 'Canteen Dada.' He had a very vivid air of overconfidence that came with many years of wholesome validation from many people. During one lunch session in our hostel canteen, while managing tasteless daal and overcooked rice, and in the middle of an argument about a finance problem, he suddenly joked that I looked like the big piece of potato on his plate. This unintelligent comment was apparently hilarious. Some tried to shush the ones laughing while giggling themselves and everyone forgot what we were discussing. It was such an obvious bullying tactic and yet, the seemingly confident, self-assured girl like

me couldn't push back. The comment wasn't really witty or factual, and yet, I was tongue-tied. I could hardly manage an exasperated eye roll and silently walked away after hurriedly finishing my lunch."

"In seventh grade, I wore a sleeveless top at school funfair and one of the boys told me my arms were disgusting. I have some dark spots in my arms because of a hormonal imbalance. He might not have realized, but his words stayed with me for years."

"I was born with a squint eye. It was always used against me in fights with my sister or classmates as the ultimate weapon. Often, the remarks were light-hearted, but I remembered them even after a surgery that corrected my eye."

"The first thing some of my relatives talked about on meeting me after long is my weight. I am told how good I will look if I lose some weight or how I will be healthier if I was thinner. When someone mean would make an unfunny joke about some chair that might break if I sat on it, I would play along. I secretly worked on my comeback but could never muster the courage to say anything out loud. I was desperate for some other tag – funny, wild, loud anything but 'Thodi moti hai.'"

✜

Have you heard of that song, *"Lakh 28 kudi da, 47 weight kudi da?"* This Honey Singh masterpiece has caused a lot of cognitive dissonance in my life. It has disturbingly objectifying lyrics that clashed directly with my feminist beliefs and yet, I have found it impossible to keep my hips stationary whenever this song has played in my vicinity. My waist which is nowhere close to 28, almost involuntarily starts grooving to this song, while I simultaneously feel guilty as a feminist and shame as an overweight woman.

To help you picture this awkward dance, imagine a jiggling belly that is a good 2 layers of chocolate cake too big. During my long Sunday bath, I often play with my belly making shapes, quite like clay. At many points in my life, I have been quite fat. 'No regular clothes fit' kind of fat. What remains today in my arms and thighs are the remains from that flourishing empire. You would think I should be mildly ashamed to make such grand announcements about the much-hated adipose tissues in my body. In this thin-crazed world, I shouldn't stutter around unfazed by the cellulite showing through my leggings. I should be apologetic about taking so much space. I should lessen the size of my self-worth along with the size of my hips. Like many others, I have done this. For many years. Constantly.

We learn to be mean to ourselves from a very young age. We are crass and impolite with ourselves. We say brutal things to ourselves constantly that are unimaginable for us to say to others. This meanness, however, is not an in-built human condition. We absorb this nastiness outside in. This is socialized and conditioned. Right from our early social groups as kids, we observe how people notice flaws in others and bully and ridicule them. *That dress doesn't suit her body type. Her eyebrows are like two caterpillars mating. Her hair looks like some bird's nest.* We all have laughed along with some hilarious body-shaming taunts – *kala kauua* for the dark ones, *mota hathi* for the fat ones, *matchstick* for the thin ones...

And through this banter and repartee, we learn that there are a wide variety of things that are wrong with our bodies – love handles, flat chests, flat bums, big bum, scanty hair, frizzy hair, dark skin, pale skin, nose that is bumpy, big, fat, or too pointy, pudgy legs, wide-shoulders, cellulite, large pores, wrinkles, freckles, birthmarks, age spots, pimples… The list of things that we should feel ashamed of is almost endless.

Sometimes, such body-shaming comments are supposedly well-meaning. Sometimes, we are told it's just for fun and we let it go even if it doesn't feel like fun. But lifelong insecurities creep in with the most unintentional comments. Irreversible hurt lingers in our hearts due to some inane comment made years ago. National Eating Disorders Association reports that about 65% of people with eating disorders say that body-shaming contributed to their condition. [28] We live in a brutal world that seems obsessed with people's appearances and remains rather ignorant about the impact this obsession has on people.

Casually commenting on someone's weight or the way their hair looks is a widely accepted form of small talk in social groups. In certain social settings, we may find it uncomfortable to comment on people's intelligence, financial situation or marital status, but we find it OK to comment on someone's weight, height or skin. While this form of casual judgement on one's appearance happens for both men and women, the scrutiny for women is far more rigorous. The research found that people compliment women colleagues on their clothes and look 4 times more than men. These casual comments, the unsolicited compliments or the harsh body shaming, all hold together this hyper-visual culture. These comments, when made in small talks or as conversation openers, might not always be negative or ill-intentioned; it might also be complimentary. But the polite, pretentious small talk has a similar psychological impact as the catcalling on the streets – they remind women that they are being watched constantly.

Add to that the culture of objectification women experience from a very young age. It is virtually impossible to avoid the item numbers, deodorant ads, magazine covers and the all-around ubiquity of images where women have been captured by a lecherous man behind the camera. Women start internalizing this gaze and start perceiving themselves as objects and adopt what psychiatrists term as "observer's perspective," for their bodies. This internalization of an outsider's perspective gets manifested as constant surveillance of one's body and results in shame and anxiety. Gradually, mirroring the meanness we see outside, we develop a pitiless inner critic constantly at work in our own heads. A nasty little bastard starts building his home inside our heads, ready to pounce on the slightest perceived ugliness in our bodies.

We might be able to overlook or even forgive ourselves for being selfish, indecisive, or unkind, but a bulge of fat or a balding head could make us obsess over it and involuntarily check, fix or cover up several times a day. This shame can happen to anyone, maybe everyone. Even the ones with great hair, those in secured relationships, those with a smile that lights up the whole room. You could be the most beautiful person in the room and yet, there could be a voice in your head that tells you that your hips are too big. And once we internalize this shame, it becomes who we are. We no longer need the bullies to tell us that we can't dress a certain way or look a certain way. We start doing that to ourselves.

In this complex, hyper-visual, hyper-connected world, one's body shame can greatly impact their life experience. It can impact who we choose to be in a relationship with, how we expect to be treated, what kinds of boundaries we draw for ourselves and how we treat others. Those who were teased and bullied suffer wounds that can bleed for a lifetime. It impacts our ability to be vulnerable and intimate and how we experience pleasure. Body shame is known to become a huge barrier to love and connection. It impacts the way we hold ourselves; it impacts the way we treat ourselves. And the statistics on body image issues are almost shocking. About 80% of 14 to 17-year-olds report being unhappy about their bodies. [29] About 73% of women who fall under the regular weight range report wanting to be thinner. [29]

If words can hurt, why don't people call out comments that they know hurt them or make them body conscious? Because the people who make you feel ashamed are the ones closest to you. Mainstream and social media may be responsible for creating unrealistic body standards for men and women of all ages, but it is the well-intentioned, ignorant and misplaced comments from people closest to us that cause long-standing harm. One research found that nearly 63% of women have been body-shamed by their mothers.

Nearly 50% of women said they'd experienced body shaming from their significant others. We don't call out such comments because while we know we are hurt;

we find it hard to say why because such repartee is so common. Most people shame others not out of spite; they do it out of habit because they don't think there's anything wrong with it. Well-meaning relatives assume the role of a counsellor and give unsolicited advice on someone's acne, weight or skin colour because they are misinformed about the impact it can have on them. Well-intentioned people can make mistakes. Loved ones can cause irreparable damage.

It is also worth wondering if so many of us feel so conscious of our bodies, why are we still so mean to others? When the phenomenon of body-shaming is so ubiquitous, we must understand that these body-shamers are people like you and me. Shouldn't suffering bring in some empathy? Shouldn't our insecurities teach us some kindness? If we know words could hurt, why are we still so careless with them with our loved ones or otherwise? The truth is, often the only way people learn to heal themselves from the brutality of others is to be a brute themselves. The only way people know how to feel better themselves when they are hurting is to hurt someone else.

Research says that people who have been body-shamed themselves are 32% more likely to body shame others. [29] Thus, the cycle of body-shaming becomes a self-perpetuating loop. While people hurt themselves, they are also guilty of laughing along with a bully's hurtful joke. When one is upset, annoyed or intimidated by someone, they default to criticizing their appearance. It feels easier to shoot for something that we know will hurt. We like targeting the physical flaws of those we resent, rather than expressing what we really feel emotionally. It often feels easier to bury underneath body-shaming comments than to address our anger or envy for someone.

But we must be able to unpack that and do better. Our words can cause someone to pause and pursue unrealistic expectations about their bodies. We know this first hand because someone's words have caused us to do the same. However well-intentioned, we must learn that the best way to comment on someone's body is to simply not. Let's find better ways of having small talks – we always have the weather, and Kangana Ranaut almost always says something stupid every week. Let's find something else to open a conversation with when we meet someone after a long time. Let's simply avoid the "oh, you have lost weight," "aww you have gained some weight," etc.

Let's be mindful of our words and aware of the impact they might have on someone. Because it is only by being kinder to others that we begin the journey of being kind to ourselves. When faced with our loved one's unintentional body shaming, we must know that intention is irrelevant. Let's protect ourselves as we would protect a child from a bully in the playground. When people comment on your weight, skin colour, hair or face in a way that is hurtful, please shut them down. Even if it is complimentary, try and not indulge. When they joke about it, please feel free to scream, even if they are family. If they get sanctimonious about how they are only trying to help you, please let them know jokes, jibes and mean-ness has helped no one. Know that you don't need to think of anything clever; just ask them to shut the fuck up.

Liking oneself and being OK with the way one looks is almost revolutionary in a world that teaches you to be mean and snarky all the time. Feeling ashamed of how we look is so normal that there was a time I almost thought that there is something odd with those who were perfectly happy with how they looked. *"Main apni favourite hoon"* is so difficult to get to and it's mostly *"main aisa kyun hoon"* that we struggle with. Self-acceptance is one of the greatest gifts we can give ourselves, but it usually comes after years of painful self-doubt and insecurities. It comes after deliberate work of finding who we are and working towards expressing it unabashedly.

Psychologists have found that midlife comes with stability and wisdom. Certain perspectives on one's identity come only with age. The amazing thing about being an adult is that you no longer need to daydream and think of how your life could be fabulous in the future when you lost all the weight or had the perfect hair. Being an adult means we can make our life the way we want, today.

Remember, when we were younger and imagined the fabulous life we could have once, we were bigger, taller, stronger, etc. We are all of that now and time is running out on our self-hating self. So, let's go and do whatever the hell we want. For me, along with the frizzy hair, the 30s brought in the ability to cut some of this bullshit from my life. I have taken mean-spirited comments to my heart all my life, but not anymore. I wear what I want, sit how I like and cut my hair as short as I want without worrying if my face would look too big. I dance to problematic rap songs with my *not-so-patli kamar* and look after my body like it is the only one I will ever have. Because guess what, it *is*.

Vitiligo – The White Demon

By Priyanka Roy Banerjee, Brussels

I was a perfectly healthy, normal kid till the age of 13. And then, my life changed forever. I started developing the little white marks on my skin. As they began spreading all around my face, I became conscious. Brought up as a single girl child by moderately pampering parents, this disfiguration was sudden and shocking to me. Not because it could change me as a person, but because it changed the way others looked at me.

I could sense people talking about me behind my back when they suddenly stopped in their tracks at the sight of me approaching. Just like it happens in the movies. I was in a co-education school, at a point in puberty when I could see friends beginning to like each other and simple friendships turning romantic. I realised that in a small suburban town, with a visible skin blight, it was impossible for me to survive or not be judged or made fun of.

My parents were flustered and ran around consulting different kinds of doctors for treatment. I gulped down medicines from all disciplines, applied ointments, observed weird dietary restrictions and hoped for miracles. The idea of meeting new people or attending family occasions seemed like nightmares. In school, I used to keep the lower part of my mouth covered with a handkerchief for most parts of the day to avoid onlookers. It was a strange affliction until we moved to Calcutta.

I felt that being a small fish in a big ocean would not demand much attention from the sharks, and it turned out to be partly true. My new school in Kolkata and new friends were not as bothered about how I looked or what I ailed from. It was quite a relief. And then I met benevolent strangers on the streets, who would initiate conversations with a 'tch, tch, how sad!' and progress to handing me visiting cards of doctors, ayurveds, hakims and stranger stuff.

I had once snapped at a man at a bus stop who tried to console me, saying, "Aap se matlab?"

I was pretty sure I did not need consolation.

Most of our relatives never let go of a chance to ask my parents, "How will you ever get her married?"

Worn out of these cannonballs, I literally fled out abroad for academics. Things have bettered since then. Having made a few amazing friends who worked on my psyche to normalise living with a disease that is not fatal or infectious. Their outpouring of love and handholding me through situations actually worked like a miracle. As it turns out, this was the only miracle I ever needed – acceptance. My partner also worked relentlessly to retrieve the self-respect that I once had. For a decade now, I have learned to live peacefully with Vitiligo. I had not chosen the disease; it was the other way round. We'd rather live in a cohabitation, accepting each other as we are and facing the world together.

Work

The one on corporations, capitalism and networking

13

What Work Means?

The one on self-image and being "just" a housewife

"I don't want to be interested in a career I know I will have to give up. What is the point in killing myself over grades and job interviews when I know that soon, I would have to leave all of these and focus on my family?"

"I have been just a housewife all my life. Looking back, I feel like I could have done something."

"I had quit my job many years back when my son was born. It was a voluntary decision, as I couldn't bear the thought of being away from him. But by the time he was 6 years old, he had a fully packed schedule himself with school, tuitions and sports. I started looking for work again and realized I had missed the bus long back. Now, I just wonder if could I have stretched some more."

In 2008, I was hired for a job which I had no skills for, not that I was employable in much else at that point. I had barely passed a 4-year long electrical engineering course, and ignorant of the tremendous privilege it was to have access to decent higher education, I had remained deeply disinterested in learning. My days went by being a real-life version of *Fukrey*, something I took a surprising amount of misplaced pride in. More than once, I got dangerously close to getting some electrical grid to collapse or some transformer to short circuit, although I am not entirely sure if transformers *can* short circuit as they are based on magnetic induction.

In any case, thanks to *Mata Rani ki Kripa* and the IT boom of the 2000s, my career took a clichéd Indian middle-class turn and I got recruited via a mass placement drive in an IT company. I was unexpectedly excited to live the Great Indian Dream of becoming the offshore counterpart to some *firang* in New York who would routinely mispronounce my name.

I remember the day I left home to join the Mysore campus of Infosys. At the airport, looking back at my dad as he waved goodbye, trying hard to hide his emotions, possibly mouthing some Bengali version of "*Jaa Simran Jaa*," for the first time, I wished he was a millionaire and I didn't have to work to earn money. As he turned back – because the free parking time at the airport was over – I realized I was stepping into the world of adults for real and it sucked. But soon, on the beautiful Infosys campus and amidst cheap and scrumptious food court meals, I found new *Fukrey* friends and a brand-new interest – software coding.

Surprisingly, this job that I took grudgingly, gave me a new self-image. We all are very quick to attach our identities to things in our lives, and I observed how work becomes a huge part of how the world looks at us and how even we look at ourselves. The 21-year-old me attached a lot of my self-worth to this job and doing it well was inexplicably important to me. I loved the challenge of writing the most optimized code, spending hours even after the training sessions, working on assignments, creating my own web pages and developing the smartest solutions. I rediscovered creativity and lateral thinking. The involvement, stimulation and pride that came along with it were life-changing. I knew I wasn't saving the world, but that intellectual stimulation, that joy of learning, was one of the most formative experiences of my life. There were days of drudgery and boredom. There were days of competition and fatigue. And yet, at the adult age of 21, to finally find a piece of work that was challenging and engaging was a spectacular thing.

Meaningful work is a human need. To be engaged in any wilful, purposeful endeavour uplifts us. All we are looking for is that beautiful thing the Greek philosopher Plato coined – *Eudaimonia*. It's a little hard to translate and it almost means 'happiness,' but it really is closer to 'fulfilment.' Work that stimulates, gives exposure to new perspectives, brings recognition and meaning, and can be fulfilling.

Rosie the Riveter, is a cultural icon from the west that many of us might have seen in memes and GIFs. Yes, that image of a woman wearing a red polka-dot bandana, showing off her arm muscle. Much like "Sharma Ji Ka Beta," which is an icon of parental pressure and rat race, Rosie is a symbol of women coming into the workforce and their financial advancement in the late 1940s. This iconography is based on the real-life phenomenon of millions of women who got into industrial work in many western countries post World War 2. As men were sent off to the battlefield, women were asked to join a variety of jobs – in construction, steel mills, transport, etc. These weren't cushy, high-paying roles. These were physically strenuous jobs like welding and riveting. And yet, the women who had taken up these jobs hesitantly due to a mid-war call to duty by the government recorded a high level of job satisfaction and very low attrition. After the war was over, millions of women spoke about the thrill and a missing sense of accomplishment that these jobs brought into their lives.

I know this idealism is dripping with *privilege*. Rosie's stylish bandana and muscle-flexing might be completely impractical to many. In India, for most women, working outside of their home is a desperate means to get by and their family's well-being depends on the money that she brings home. But the impact of work in our lives is not always just monetary, although that is a big part of why many of us work.

And one of the many people who brought in this perspective was Gayatri Vasudevan, who heads Labournet, an NGO based in Bangalore that works on skill development for men and women in economically struggling communities. The primary focus of Gayatri's group is to better the earning potential of people by enrolling them on skill development courses. Most organizations that work with Labournet under their CSR programs evaluate the programs based on the earning potential of women post completion of the learning modules.

Having worked with hundreds of men and women over decades across skill areas, industries and sectors, Gayatri was convinced of how irrespective of the seriousness, level of advancement or type of job, all work was eventually an opportunity for women to explore a new facet of their personality. Having witnessed thousands of women complete courses like computer basics, accounting or beauty salon services, Gayatri said that the biggest impact she has seen work bring in the lives of women is not money or security. It is the sense of liberation.

Work, for these women, is a window to the outside world, it brings in a fresh set of perspectives, a new set of friends. Exposure to people and ideas beyond their families and neighbours has a deep bearing on their worldview and self-esteem. Knowing the ways of the world brings self-reliance and a sense of self to women's lives, which possibly is of as much value, if not more, than the power that earning money brings.

Millions of women in India – engineers, MBAs, post-graduates – do not have professional careers. India has the *highest* proportion of overeducated, over-qualified housewives in the world. I wonder if this statistic has reached Ekta Kapoor and we could get better quality television, but I digress. Defying global trends, the proportion of working-age women who were either employed or looking for work has reduced from 33% in the 1990s to 18.2% in 2018.

Unlike South Korea, Japan and China, other Asian countries with a similar patriarchal cultural paradigm, in India, women's participation in the labour force *decreased* with the economic growth of the country. For many women, if money is not a constraint and the family can get by with the income of the male earning members, taking up a profession is deemed unnecessary. Even today, in many middle-class homes in India, women working outside of their homes is considered an act of rebellion. Having a career is looked at as an avenue to get exposed to dangerous new ideas and new people. A job allows women to legitimately cross the literal or metaphorical "*Lakshman rekha*" of their homes. Life beyond these boundaries could be a world full of possibilities and freedom for them. And for many, this possibility is dangerous.

Women need to be lucky enough to get their parents', in-laws', husband's, kids', fufaji's, chachaji's permission to be able to work. If she is lucky enough to have a small window to pursue professional work, it becomes something to bide her time between mealtimes with the family. Work, in its most essential form – to absorb oneself, to find meaning and self-worth – remains an unknown concept in many women's lives.

Many economists and feminists have tried to put a dollar value on the unpaid labour done by women across the world. Having a home, keeping together a family and raising kids are extremely meaningful work. The economies of industrialized countries would collapse in a day if women didn't do the work they do in their homes for free. The reason that such incredibly important work done by women is ignored or undervalued is that it doesn't earn *paisa*.

For millions of women, the work done within the four walls of their home is unappreciated, repetitive and intellectually unstimulating. Her selfless work which enables her kids and her husband to go out in the world is hardly noticed by the ones she loves the most. It is taken for granted and brings no special social standing. The economic dependence of women on a male provider also puts them at a massive disadvantage and contributes to much of their oppression in the world. In domestic violence cases, adultery cases or even in cases of general incompatibility, women are unable to break an unhealthy marital relationship because of the harsh economic hardship that follows.

The value of labour in this world is indeed skewed. The fact is, work has no intrinsic value. It is worth what one can push the system to pay for. In this capitalistic model, the worth of a piece of work is how much it pays or how much power that work gives over other people. What follows is that much of our self-worth comes from how much we earn.

For men, their "package," which could mean both the size of their penis or the 0's in their salary, is a huge part of their self-worth. Just a quick google search will reveal millions of blogs dedicated to how to enhance both packages. Of course, much of it is internalized and subconscious, but one is taught to instinctively connect *value* to *money* in this world and the value of our labour feels a lot less when it doesn't earn us money.

This is the culture that makes our restful, joyful hours feel wasteful and glamourises hustle and productivity. Housewives feel the same pinch. There is an unspoken stigma to the term "housewife," and in common parlance, it has been changed to "home-maker," although the world hasn't yet started looking at the work women do – the nurturing of the kids, the care for the elderly and the continuous emotional support for their husbands with any more reverence.

Naina, who I met during my research, introduced herself as 'just a housewife' when I met her a couple of years back. She was in her late 40s, a mother of two teenage kids and lived with her husband in a suburban community in Hyderabad. She had an infectious, loud laugh and one could instantly know that she must have been fabulous as an Electronics Sales representative in the job she'd had almost two decades back. She told me she quit because she didn't need her income and the kids needed her to be present 24X7 in their lives.

As we got talking, I complained about my job – the excessive travel, exhausting politics and long hours. With each complaint I had, Naina was beaming with suggestions and solutions. I complained about having a travel-intensive job. She told me how much she loved sleeping in hotel beds during the annual sales conferences. I spoke about long working hours; she talked about a sales pitch she worked on that cracked one of the biggest clients for her company. She still cared deeply about the job she quit many years back, reminiscing fondly about her colleagues, awards and promotions that came with it.

She confessed she missed working but conceded that if she decided to work again, there were some difficult choices that lay ahead of her. Most of those choices she simply didn't want to make. Naina then spoke passionately about multiple social groups she was a part of now: her kitty circle, mommy group from her kid's school, her residential colony ladies club and many others. In her own way, she seemed to have found a way to be an organizer as she organized the annual society events, multiple parents' meetups and more. She also teaches yoga to her friends, decorates her home artistically on every occasion and makes the most delicious cakes.

How do you define such a person? Saying that she is 'just a housewife' is like building a dam over an ocean. We will overlook so many aspects of her life by describing her only as a housewife. But that was now her identity; not just for the world but for herself too.

Tens of middle-aged women I met nervously laughed when they mentioned that their husbands didn't allow them to work after they had kids. For some of them, it was voluntary as good quality childcare was expensive and difficult to find. They argued that the family didn't need their income and that being a full-time mother was the best contribution they could make to the family. In many of these conversations, I got a slight glimpse of their guilt and insecurities as they wondered late in their life what their life amounted to. Many said pensively, "*kuch kar lena tha.*" Somehow, all the years gone by caring for the kids and family didn't amount to enough for her. "*Kuch kar sakte the*" remains a nagging thought amongst 45-50-year-olds as they feel a pang of something missing in their lives. A problem with no name, indeed. [31]

Millions of women who spend a seemingly perfect life, making *garam* rotis for their husbands and cleaning the runny nose of their thankless children, often speak of loneliness, frustration and a yearning for a possibility that they felt was left unexplored. Housewives accounted for the second-highest percentage of all suicide victims in India in 2018, after daily-wage labourers, according to the latest National Crime Records Bureau (NCRB) report. In 2018, 22,937 housewives committed suicide — *more than double* the number of farmers who committed suicide. While the latter got its due share of media attention and political momentum, mainstream media stayed out of women's suicide cause entirely, except on rare reportage on mistreatment by in-laws and harassment for dowry.

Even though a larger theme is common between farmer suicides and housewives' suicides – a sense of entrapment due to the gender diktats. On one hand, as married women are being pushed to suicide under the weight of being an 'ideal' wife, daughter-in-law and mother, on the other hand, farmers end their lives, crushed under the sole masculine responsibility of feeding large families through drought or floods, with no one to share the burden, financially or emotionally. It's all a part of the same rot – a gendered way of looking at work.

Many would say, we are starting to see this change. Across matrimony sites and ladies' clubs, we are starting to hear of this growing demand for *"job-wali bahu."* Today, everybody seems to know that women need a bit of money. But a career is an entirely different matter. Veiled as progress, this phenomenon doesn't come from an intention of women's empowerment. As many frankly concede *"ek aadmi ke kamai se zindagi nahi chalti."* We are starting to expect women to contribute to the family monetarily as families in modern consumeristic societies need a higher inflow of money to sustain themselves.

You would think, the end justifies the means, right? How does it matter if it is from a place of empowerment or compulsion? Eventually, we would have more women in the workforce, which would mean they would get exposure to the world of new ideas and perspectives? But there is a massive flaw. These families that gloat about being "modern" enough to allow their daughters-in-law to work are not objective enough to expect their sons to contribute to the household. This leaves women constantly multi-tasking and exhausted.

In upper-class homes, "working women," who get paid for their work outside of their home, hire other women as maids to do their housework, which they would otherwise have done for free if they weren't working. The men in the homes have nothing to do with the housework or the maid. The mental load of missing a meeting if the nanny doesn't turn up, or the guilt that comes with realizing that curd is over when the guests ask for it, still comes on the woman of the house. Women accept this as their destiny. They are held back and burdened by these superhuman expectations and they internalize this as their personal failure.

Even mothers in middle-class Indian homes are starting to teach their girls to be independent and pursue a profession. They speak to them with a yearning for a career they could never have and teach them to learn the tricks of the world from their fathers. They have even started insisting more on studying than learning how to sew and cook. But mothers are unable to give their daughters the image needed to visualize that future with a full-time job, well-fed kids and a clean home. There are no role models who seem to have the best of both worlds – a happy home with kids and a flourishing career.

Many girls grow up feeling free and equal to boys, riding bicycles, competing in geometry, and going to college away from their homes. But this does not prepare them for the role they are expected to play as married women with kids when they are forced to adjust and make some very hard choices in their lives. That's why often in their adult lives, women are starting to feel so out of breath. We grow up wanting to be like our dads – powerful and ambitious – but once we have a career like him, which is travel-intensive, high paying and physically and mentally exhausting, the world wants us to be like our mothers – adjusting, dutiful and nurturing. Our family's *sukh-shanti* depends on our disproportionate emotional and physical labour.

Women today are pulled in several directions; they must multitask because they are constantly told to balance. 'Having it all" is the constant ideal fed to modern women and it comes with the often unspoken "doing it all." There is also a general mistrust of women's judgement. If she is a full-time homemaker, she is judged as lazy and lacking talent. If she is a full-time career woman, she is expected to be a full-time ninja as well. But we forget that multi-tasking takes away from our ability to give our all to something – to focus on and master one singular thing. Our self-worth comes from achievements and the pursuit of excellence. Be it baking the 7-layered cake for our kid's birthday party, flawlessly hosting a party or making a winning sales pitch, the big feel-good accomplishments in our lives come from putting ourselves single-mindedly into one thing. The world doesn't allow that single-mindedness to women, making us feel less of a woman if we are unable to balance it all. Normalcy, flaws, humanity, exhaustion and time-outs are just not accorded to women.

When it comes to work – outside or in-home – the trick is to have unabashed pride in it. Whatever we choose to spend our time doing, whether it is our dream job of wildlife photography or a conventional role that needs us to make excel sheets or make that flawless Mac and Cheese for our kid's birthday party; whatever we do, we should be able to immerse ourselves in it with purpose and infuse it with our own selves. Drop the pursuit of "having it all" and pursue instead the idea of "the life I love."

The promotion, package or corner office does not define us. There is no single tag – corporate leader or homemaker – that defines us. Our labour, either paid or unpaid, is an expression of who we are. How we contextualize this in our own heads is important for our well-being. Eventually, it will take us many years of introspection and self-doubt to find work that is fulfilling to us or form an identity that truly resonates with us and fills us with pride and joy. When we are asked, "What do you do?" let's say all the things we enjoy doing and not simply "Just a housewife," or "I work with ABC company." Let the men worry about the packages; let us women redefine how work is valued. And let's not shrink ourselves into our job description.

14

Corporate *Taam Jhaam* – A Game of Toxicity and Money

The one on affirmative action and feminine leadership

"Since I have gone back to the office after my maternity leave, I just constantly worry about my daughter. Sometimes, I find myself totally distracted at work when she is ill. I have always been a top performer at my job, but I don't think I can continue this way for long."

"I once had a boss who just looked at me weirdly. He was a respected man with rich experience. But there was something in the way that he stared at me, sometimes my chest, while I spoke that made me feel very uncomfortable. I started dressing differently and stopped speaking during meetings to avoid his attention."

"I was the only woman in the team. During team outings, I used to be the one to go back to my room early. I was not called for the after-party, not that I wished to join myself. I knew it would not be fun for me."

"I was told by my boss in an office party, in a drunken state, possibly jokingly that I was the 'diversity hire.' I felt so embarrassed. I knew I would have never been respected for my work there."

As someone with an over-active imagination, I often visualize that a few decades ago, a grand committee of powerful men chaired by Salman Khan, Donald Trump and Jack Welch announced "*Welcome to gender equality, ladies! Let us show you around,*" and took us all on a field trip to show the new-age, supposedly gender-equal world.

They said, *"Congratulations! We no longer burn the witches or the widows. Here are the constitutions of countries based on "equal rights of all men," but remember the doctrine of coverture that nullifies a woman's legal identity after marriage still stays in some form in many countries in 2022. Best you don't think too much about your legal rights because convictions on rape and dowry cases would still be less than 25%. The banks and the stock markets we created with capitalistic, divisive, cut-throat, hierarchal systems are over there; have a good time working in them for 70 hours a week. But don't forget, being pretty and raising children will still be your primary role! Come on, smile, woman!"*

In about 80% of the conversations I have had about this book with class/caste-privileged lot, I have had a '*but women today are everywhere, haan!*' line thrown at me. Almost as if I am too late to write this. "What is so much *shor* about diversity now?" I am asked. The big bad Patriarchy, if still alive, must be in people's homes in small towns or in streets and crowded buses with crass hooligans. In the posh corporate offices with fancy décors, highly qualified individuals and foamy coffee, there exists no discrimination. I am told that discrimination is almost an imaginary concept in professional corporate structures and in reality, "strong" women have always risen to the top and they are living proof of equality in the workplace. Look at Indira Nooyi, look at Chanda Kochar, look at Sheryl Sandberg, look at <fill in the gap with a woman CEO>

When the few names of women leading big companies dry up, *"I have had a woman boss,"* comes out. As the argument now continues in an audibly higher pitch, they bring in the big guns – Meritocracy. The singular word that is handy to cut across all discussions of equality. All the affirmative action that we see corporations espouse today are PR stunts, they baulk, and those are simply professional free hands to undeserving women. Any further push for equality will cause imbalance and will be an unnatural structure created by those loud feminist women. Women of today are already a bit *too* equal, a bit too free, a bit too much, they say with a squeaky voice.

The implicit argument covered underneath big jargon and skewed data is simply that the best person for any high-paying, powerful job in this world is a man. Women still occupy less than 15% of top corporate jobs. So, if structural inequities don't exist, is it our incompetence and or laziness that hold us back? The fact that women make only 3% of corporate CEOs, 7% of top earners, 14% of executive officers and 16% of board members is simply because we are slacking off, I curiously wonder. I am then told, in a somewhat awkward tone which barely hides the obvious condescension, that this under-representation in top roles is driven by women working fewer hours. It is possibly the result of personal choices, or it might be because women don't negotiate or network. The playing field is already levelled and the mostly male line-up in the alleys of power is simply based on merit, personal choices or inherent under-confidence of women.

Despite an overwhelming proportion of women experiencing a tumultuous and often sporadic professional journey rift with sacrifices, exhaustion and guilt, we continue to find comfort in the minority of success stories. As if women have recently cropped up on the face of the earth and do not form most of the human population that even their minor participation in the echelons of power must be celebrated. The glorious examples of women shattering the glass ceiling and reaching top positions of power are inspiring, but in no way is it statistically significant for us to hang our boots and pat our backs. A large number of women claim they are often the only woman in a room or amongst the very few. Women report discrimination in the workplace, but being the only woman is a worse experience. [36] There is a widely reported motherhood penalty women pay in corporate jobs that demonstrate how workplaces are designed around the clockwork of the male career, and if women took a break, they are ostracised and left behind. [33]

The pay gap exists very visibly across all spheres of work and industries [34] with the median gross hourly salary for men being ₹242.49, compared to ₹196.3 for women, meaning men earned ₹46.19 more than women for every hour of work. This despite women sharing the significantly higher proportion of unpaid labour at home.

[34] Unconscious bias that impacts hiring, progression and retention of women in the workplace [35] is widely reported and slowly being unravelled in all its forms. This is while women say they need to work harder than men to prove themselves; that they feel constant pressure to never make a mistake and feel the corporate culture does not suit them. Women are increasingly finding the corporate structures too difficult to navigate while constantly fighting the unconscious bias and having to carry the burden and guilt of household work they drop off. [33]

Structural inequalities exist and glaringly so in corporations, public service, entertainment, sports and in every field of work. The assumption that as people swipe their ID cards in the morning to enter the office building, they become a different person with a new understanding of justice and equity is dubious. The belief that the swanky elevators we take to reach our high-rise office floors have some magic that makes us forget the years of patriarchal conditioning and misogynistic cultural paradigms is misguided. Prejudice and stereotypes are not like walls that are visible to everybody; they are like curtains that exist camouflaged.

In her stunning book, Invisible Women, Feminist author Carolina Perez gives nuanced, eye-opening, worldview-shaking examples of ways in which women have been kept out of public policy, history, art, media, research and every single sphere of our world. What we know of the human world and its history, how we do research on human bodies and create cures for our diseases, how we code artificial intelligence and plan our future, how we form policies and represent ourselves in art and media – EVERY.SINGLE.WAY in whichever way we think, feel and imagine, it takes the human male as the default. It is simply not a world that has been created thinking of women or even a diverse population.

Over the last few decades, much has changed. The life that my Dida lived as someone married off at 17 has been very different from the life my Ma lived, and my own life has moved quite off the trend graph. But if we look deeply, have the institutions which were built on the foundations of patriarchy, casteism and classism really changed? Have the principles, so ingrained in our systems, changed?

It's easy to talk about participation and representation, but what is difficult is to right the wrongs and build a truly equitable world. That needs fundamental shaking up of the systems within the sphere of work as well the larger culture we live within. We want women in the auto sector, army, sales and all those traditionally male-infested white-collar territories. But are these industries being changed to be ready for women? In corporations today, it is glamourous to say that we are "gender-blind," but our dreamy approach assumes the world is gender blind. For women's equal representation and participation to happen, it must become culturally acceptable for men to deprioritize their career prospects to support the women in their lives to succeed professionally. Friends must ridicule those men who "disallow" their wives from working after getting married. Neighbourhood aunties should gossip about the family that does not support their daughter's or daughter-in-law's passion.

When we ensure that there are a greater number of women represented at the top, it has shown to have a multiplier effect. Companies with stronger feminine participation on boards have proven to be more profitable. And most importantly, visible role models have emerged to inspire younger women and encourage mid-senior level women to keep climbing the slippery slopes of the corporate ladder. In principle, many of these policies have shown to work and have had a far-reaching effect on bettering balance, not just in the workplace but in our communities and homes. Having more women come into professions and roles, which have traditionally been marred by discrimination and a culture that kept women out, is a great first step.

But affirmative action by many corporations sometimes ends up becoming tokenistic. For truly equal participation of women in the workforce, work must be equally rewarding and joyous for women, not just equally accessible. Without the structural changes in things that craft our culture, diversity will simply become a corporate strategy as Angela Davis, the much-loved feminist researcher, pointed out years ago. The flawed institutions will continue to function as they are, but simply with more diverse faces. It will become a difference that doesn't create much difference.

In my decade-long professional career across multiple industries, roles and companies, I have been inundated by motivational messages and confidence-building workshops. The number of books, blogs and talks that tell women they are doing it all wrong in their high-impact roles might be more than the sum of women actually *in* high-impact roles. We teach women a lot of things – we criticize them for being too sensitive and tell them to never cry in the office. We teach them to not say sorry too often, to not start emails with "just wanted to or just checking." We tell them to not be ambivalent about authority and yield their power. We show them research that says men apply for jobs they are not fully qualified for and women should too. We tell them men have firmer handshakes and they should try that too. In a variety of small and big ways, we tell them we want women to act more like men. We tell them that what the men do at work is innately superior and that's the way to succeed in this world. And hence, the few women who do get into the hallowed walls of corporate power circles, with access to a slight hint of influence, must make themselves more like men – brash, aggressive, stoic, ballsy, mean and detached.

But there's a huge, gaping and embarrassingly obvious hole in these tactics that tell women to unleash their inner beast in the battleground for corporate power – it assumes that the current benchmark of leadership and the corporate culture it breeds is ideal. Any observant, rational person can spend a day in these dreamy, glass-walled big offices with multi-functional coffee machines and exotic wall-arts and realize how underneath all the *taam-jhaam,* these places are simply a heady mix of politics, jealousy and redundant emails.

Most workplaces are run by unnecessary hierarchies, cut-throat competition and brutal normal curves that crush personal identities. These places that glorify humans as "resource," demand loyalty and submission instead of creativity and compassion. They reward confidence over competence and profitability over purpose. A 2016 study involving over 6,000 employees from multiple cities in India, working across sectors and companies, found that 80% of respondents exhibited symptoms of anxiety while 55% had symptoms of depression. [32] Please re-read those percentages! It's time to question our perception of what "good leadership" constitutes. Because the benchmark now is literally driving people mad.

Equality is good. But it is often equated with sameness. Having equal representations and the exact same rights is critical, but adopting the exact same cultural paradigms which dictate masculine behaviour would keep the systems intact. We would simply have more of what we have now – people corrupted by power, divided by hierarchies and a system that is built on inequal, inhuman frameworks.

We will clamour for women's entry into the army and frontline combat roles, but while we do that, we also need women in powerful positions who have the influence to reimagine these structures of national armies that cause unimaginable human miseries and start building a world devoid of wars and armies. We will put all our might to break the glass ceiling and enter the boardrooms, but we also need women who would help reimagine the remuneration structures, the inhuman working hours and change the cut-throat, competitive environments of corporations which do little for human wellbeing. Sameness will help us trick patriarchy into including more women under its umbrella, but it won't beat it. It won't beat what patriarchy does best – divide and crush.

Our love affair with corporate hierarchy and power has its origins in our ancestral primate instincts for contest, dominance and pecking orders. But these have always been obsessions and addictions of men in the patriarchal order. Women have traditionally been outside of these games of status and power. Which is possibly our biggest flaw and yet, our biggest strength. While women in many ways exhibit a slightly ambivalent approach to authority, this makes them open to cooperative relationships and ventures which has gained increased importance in today's globally connected modern world. Across various research, people feel female leaders were more compassionate and empathetic, even more ethical. [37] So, instead of asking women leaders to be more like men – entitled, incompetent yet confident – isn't it time we asked male leaders to be more like women – empathetic, collaborative and vulnerable? Is it then time to re-imagine what corporations could look like?

Gender is the axis on which this unsustainable and mindless structure could be completely flipped and re-built on. Having a balance of masculine and feminine ethos at the workplace can eventually make the office coffee smell better, figuratively and literally. Re-looking at this structure through rose-tinted glasses (pun-intended) of human values, empathy and kindness could re-shape it. At the end of the day, I am not an economist or a behavioural expert, but I am simply a woman with tens of unread motivational emails that tell me to turn *Rambo* at work, standing in front of a male-centric corporate culture, asking it nicely to be a bit less toxic!

For better or for worse, our world today is run by corporations. Not in the simplistic way that Whatsapp forwards claim Mukesh Ambani is the real Prime Minister of India, but in a complex, layered and deeply interconnected way. Our world is run by money that is held by very few. Our country, and most of the western world, is run by a model that is theoretically called political capitalism. It is where a sinister nexus between large capital holders and political powerhouses forms an economy and a social order that no longer has the self-correcting mechanisms of free markets. And yet, what religion was in the 17th century, capitalistic corporations are in the 21st century – all-powerful, unquestionable and sacrosanct.

We take immense pride in the power of the free market and blindly believe in its incorruptibility. We swear by the ruthless objectivity of "profits" and "growth" and pardon whatever goes in the name of *dhandha*, because eventually, businesses are supposed to be driving livelihoods and growth, and what could be a bigger goal than the GDP of nations? This fundamental lens of keeping profit at the core of corporations makes it impossible to re-imagine it.

If Coca-Cola starts making its cola less addictive, thinking of the billions of kids' health it harms every year, how will it make money for its shareholders? But contrary to Milton Friedman's maxim, the business of business should not just be business. The business of business should be to create value for society. Shareholder value alone should not be the yardstick. Instead, we should make stakeholder value, or better yet, social value, the benchmark for a company's performance.

Political, economic and cultural systems don't operate in isolation, distinct from each other. They are interconnected and collectively form our human experience. These systems have been created by people, mostly men, but still humans, people, homo sapiens. We need a change in who is making these systems, who are holding them together and who are imagining them. As women, we should know that we can imagine this world differently. We are in a critical time in history where women holding some form of power, must identify and manifest their own feminine values, not as they were defined by patriarchy, culture or by the media. We should embrace vulnerability and sentimentalism. We should proudly cry, make a scene, hoot and hug.

The stoic, clinical, sterile workplaces are a thing of the past century. In a world where creativity, human connections and innovation are at the centre of all businesses, insincerity and cutthroats just can't be part of our workplace culture. How about we value authenticity over stoicism? For the longest time, we simply wanted more women in the room – more women with decision-making power, more women with a voice. And we still do. We do need the old structures dominated by men – governments, businesses, art, everything really – to get their *god-damned* act together and make more space for women. By affirmative action, policies, laws and more, we must get more women *into* the system. But it's simply not enough for us to become CEOs and leaders if we don't demonstrate a new type of leadership, based on kindness and authenticity. It is simply not enough for us to find our space within the system of power. We must also use that power to change the flaws in the system.

#A Manifesto

Simply being a woman in a leadership role is a revolution. All women going out and working are silently changing a millennia-old structure that was just not made thinking of us. I do deserve a massive part of the credit for my professional growth and educational background. But the thoughts I think, the way I can live my life has not just been mine but of millions of women all through history who pushed their boundaries and questioned the oppressive status quo. They bled until they could no longer hold the rope thrown down to us and passed it on to other brave women who did the same. I intend to continue that glorious tradition of sisterhood – to hold out the metaphorical rope in my family, office and community for other women to cling on and climb up.

I will always carry a lipstick, pain relief medicine and a tampon because one never knows which amazing woman one would get to help and befriend.

I will never fight with other women for the breadcrumbs that patriarchy leaves behind for women. I will take women along and claim a big bite out of the pie.

I will hold onto my authenticity, vulnerability, and compassion always and would not mould myself into a template of unemotional, cut-throat, and hierarchical leadership.

The Last Word

15

On Re-Imaging the World Through a Feminist Lens

I have often struggled between the two options of being kind or being right. In a hyper-polarized world, it seems like one cannot be both. And boy, does it feel good to be right! To shame those who are wrong in their wrongful wrongness. It feels so good to be sure about things. It feels so good to occupy some unbreachable height of moral superiority and look down on those who are flawed or ambivalent.

But if we are completely honest, there is often a gap between our intellectual beliefs and our actual real-world behaviour. In that space between theory and our everyday lives, we all are a little flawed, selfish, inconsistent and lazy. As women, we are not just victims of patriarchy, but we also, knowingly or otherwise, propagate it. We negotiate with the power structures in our own lives with the power we hold – the means we have.

It has taken me some time, but I have come to forgive myself and others for this inner schism. I have come to realize that we are never going to be perfectly moral, selfless, uncomplicated beings. But our humanity lies in our constant striving. It lies in realizing that we cannot even begin to challenge other people's attitudes without first examining our own set of prejudices. It lies in the understanding that if we deny others the autonomy to form opinions based on inputs they have, we limit our autonomy in doing that too.

Being set in our way of thinking is laziness. It is like letting a thick layer of cholesterol build around our minds due to our lack of curiosity. It is incredibly limiting to believe that our perspectives are the whole truth and there could be no other way of thinking. So, being super right and ultra-sure of ourselves in this world with complicated truths and multi-dimensional realities is simply insincere.

It is not difficult to see this complexity when it comes to experiences of women, Dalits, disabled or queer folks who have been outside of traditional power structures. There remains so much that is not recorded or depicted about the powerless in this world. Our perception of reality simply does not factor them in with nuance or layers. It is the powerful who write history, movies and books. We do not hear, know or research the powerless – their lives, health, sexuality, ambitions, flaws, and perspectives. The experiences of those without power are not the norm or the default in this world, while they form a large part of humanity.

We live in a world where women are known to be someone's wife or girlfriend. We live in a world where queer people are defined only by their strife and struggles. In the movies we have grown up watching, male heroes are characterized by their hopes, dreams, flaws and desires. Even villains have layered back stories and nuance in their characterization. But female characters are written with a tokenistic one-dimensionality that only talks about either their physical beauty, relationship or pitiable struggles.

Women and their experiences are so systematically excluded that we do not see women as whole people with complex inner worlds. We simply do not think of women; we do not look at them deeply. Women themselves don't look inward to see who we truly are, what are some of our failures, what hurts and what brings us joy. As we discover and experience the world from a man's perspective, we learn to delete our experiences from our own consciousness. We learn to trivialize our pain; we learn to ignore our discomfort. We do not stop and question any of it.

I am often told that I am blinded by ideology. I cannot see the world objectively because I am too feminist! Over many years of trying to decipher what exactly being "too feminist" means, I have come to understand that it is simply seeing the world from a woman's perspective. Being too feminist is considering women's experiences as real and alive and not theoretical and ideological. It is to not look at the male perspective as default. When our objectivity is male, I am glad to reject it.

I am also often told that Feminism is a western concept from the 1960s, and in today's world, it is irrelevant. The days of the angry, hysterical, bra-burning feminists are well and over. Women are no longer the weaker sex in a marriage, they no longer cook or meekly accept their husband's demands and today, they get all the rights and divorces they want. Gender equality has already been achieved.

The reality, of course, stands quite far from it. One of the truest tests of having power is not just having a voice and a say in things that matter. It is having the permission to be layered, flawed, mediocre and human. And nowhere in the world have we been able to achieve that. Women are simply not accorded their humanity as much as we accord it to men. Whenever we have come even close to women's subjective realities being mainstreamed, we made many people very uncomfortable. It altered many dearly held values of ours; it challenged our beliefs and our way of life.

Much like the stock market, patriarchy still thrives in our world despite robbing millions of people. We keep giving it bailouts as governments do with big crony capitalistic companies. We end up redefining patriarchy, negotiating with it, making our own small changes in our limited life contexts because the gendered way of our lives is "too big to fail." We muzzle our curiosity and never question the structures of heteronormativity, marriage, beauty standards, toxic workplace culture and more. We accept the world as seen from the men's POV. We accept the world that is deeply hierarchical, brutally violent and largely masculine. We focus on productivity, efficiency and hustle while forgetting creativity, humanity and joy. A humane, empathetic and arguably feminine approach can save the world, and yet, we simply deny it's a possibility.

There is a very interesting theory in the study of human psychology called The Ultimatum Game. This has been studied in a large variety of circumstances, but the basic principle is that suppose you have two people Alpha and Bina, and you give Alpha an amount of $10. You empower Alpha to choose to give however much he wants to give to Bina. And the rule is Bina now has the option to either accept or reject this. If Bina accepts whatever Alpha gives, say $1, without any negotiation, the game ends and Alpha gets $9 and Bina gets $1. In case Bina rejects the offer Alpha makes, no one gets anything. If Bina is perfectly rational and selfish, she takes whatever Alpha offers, as for her, something is better than nothing. But if Bina is somewhat irrational or thinks of others who might follow her and rejects an unequal distribution, she would be able to bargain a better deal. Because when Alpha knows they are dealing with a person who would not accept an unequal distribution, they will offer $3 or $4. And just like that, B can extract more from A. Rejecting the offer of unequal distribution is, in effect, paying to punish the dictator or Alpha. When sufficient people reject a system of unequal distribution, it becomes more just and equitable for all.

Millennial women have seen a lot of change in their lives. We had a childhood before the internet, we have seen a world where we did not have access to information and we now live in a world where we are not sure this unbridled access is all that good a thing. We have the objectivity needed to look at this world and its evolution and decide for ourselves what parts we want to retain and which parts we want to reject. We are at the cusp of re-writing the indelible rules of marriage, motherhood, beauty and work. We also have the access, connections and language to change the world. And we must.

So, yes, I am blinded by the belief that there is a better way of arranging our world. I wonder what it would look like to reimagine a broken system. How can women in powerful positions today relook at systems? How can ordinary women in their everyday lives reimagine some of our most dearly held but flawed power structures of caste, class and gender binary? I am blinded by the hope that the way we have organized our world could be relooked through a kinder, inclusive and feminist lens and made to work better for everyone. Because that is the thing about being radical and uncompromising – we hold the potential to change the world like those brave women did decades back. It is through this that we can re-start a revolution in our everyday lives against stereotypes, sexism, biases and violence, but mostly against insecurities, unaddressed guilt and not knowing ourselves.

What is important is that we constantly do the work and don't expect all our education and unlearning to come from activists or our marginalized friends or colleagues. What is important is that we are open to changing our minds and being kind to those who do. What is important is that we don't cage ourselves in either rebellion or obedience and instead, develop a mind of our own that doesn't live in reaction to the world outside; one that forges its own path with freedom, conviction and joy. And live a life that is not simply filled with unbending ideas that are for or against something, but with principles that are built from scratch with experience.

Albert Einstein once said, possibly in a very different context, "Never stop questioning. Curiosity and revolution both have a reason to exist for their own purpose." We cannot but stop and wonder if there are better ways of arranging the world out there. There are definitely better ways of arranging our inner worlds. The mystery of life, the interconnectedness of history and future and the interconnectedness of capitalism, casteism, gender and classism demand our curious questioning. It is important that we connect and form patterns, not just to understand the world better but to understand ourselves more deeply. Our reality is a marvellous structure. It is formed by our perception, nature, social structures, conditioning and many things together. Our ability to dissect these, understand these and when needed, dismantle their power will form the very basis of how we experience our life and spend our limited time on this planet.

Our world might be more polarized than ever today, but it is also more connected than ever. While it holds the potential to poison and close our minds to everything that we do not comprehend, it also has the potential to give us a deeper understanding of our lives through shared experiences. The true magic of living in a connected world is in finding solidarity. At any time, when we find the courage to share stories from our inner world, there would be someone out there who will grab our hands and remind us that we are not as alone as we feared. There's magic in that feeling. To be seen by someone who understands gives us permission to keep going.

And while Feminism has been known to be a movement primarily concerned with gender, I now know that in its very essence, it has always been focused on something much bigger – kindness. What makes us revolutionary is not our comprehension and perfect, concise worldview, but it is our compassion and empathy. It is in our ability to hold space for someone, it is in our humility to accept mistakes and do better, it is in our ability to acknowledge our privilege and power and in holding it for someone else.

It did not feel like it when I was younger, but I had, in fact, won the ovarian lottery, not of unbridled money or access, but the lottery of hope-tinted glasses that I saw the world with. I was protected from the inequal, inhuman realities of the world with stories, music and humour. As I grew up, those glasses had a lot of scratches and cracks, and at some point, they were altogether abandoned. But through the process of writing and researching this book, I found small pieces of cello tapes scattered across the stories of women I met through which I could mend that ignored broken piece of hope.

Through the online community of everyday revolution, I continue to find this incredible joy of meeting women every day. They hype me up, bring me back on planet earth, guide me, and critique me all with a sense of familiarity and candour that is difficult to understand. When women open up about their lives with honesty and authenticity, they wonderfully bring more women into their lives and enrich all their lives spectacularly.

Women often forget that they are people with feelings, power and identity of their own. They forget that their life has value for its own sake and not in relation to others. Living our most authentic lives – knowing the harms done to us and the ones we did to ourselves – is one of the few time-tested ways of having stable adult lives. Our experiences and conditioning define us and make us who we are. They are the most exciting stories in our world. To others, the story of our life might seem silly, small and mundane but to us, in our life and its context, it has deep meaning and bearing. We all live our lives like a fish in a tank; we only look at the tank from the inside, not understanding its full size and scale.

This is why we must use our personal experiences and the stories of other women to understand the larger construct of human society. These stories can be the window to the world and its functioning. It could give us an insight into how things work and it could give us the required courage and conviction to fight for change.

Sisterhood is the oldest tool in history that women have used so deftly across centuries to make sense of this patriarchal world that does not represent their subjective reality. It is the tool that is as important today as it ever has been. There is an indescribable beauty in finding our own tribe in this random, cluttered, noisy world. There is an inexplicable comfort in connecting with someone, hearing their story and saying, "Hey, that happened with me too!" or "I thought it was just me!"

An understanding of our context and empathy for other people's context makes us better people, but more importantly, happier people. This is why it is important that we use the magic of a blank paper or the internet to narrate the life story of ours. It is important that we look back at our life story and write it in our own words. Our life stories are not stories when we are living them. They become stories in our memories and nostalgia. It is only when we remember that we finally make sense of certain experiences. It is when we make peace with ourselves – with what is inside our head and heart – we are ok with the most embarrassing thoughts and the most wicked deeds. Our past then becomes our fuel. We no longer need to second guess or manufacture feelings.

Our lives deserve a glorious memoir even if we are the only ones reading it. Write your stories so that someone might feel understood, even if that someone is just you. As the Buddhist saying goes, "The most fundamental harm we do to ourselves is to remain ignorant by not having the courage or the respect to look at our own lives honestly and gently."

Growing up in a politically left-aligned Bengali home, I had thought of 'revolution' as something to do on the streets, out in the world. But as an adult, I realized that the most radical revolution in this world happens inside our minds and hearts. It is transformative to be able to deconstruct our childhood, it is radical to feel entitled to nourishing relationships, and it is revolutionary to seek meaningful, non-toxic jobs. I hope, through the perspectives and stories in this book, you find what you need to start and continue you own inner revolution. May you find clarity to choose, the courage to follow through, and joy in changing your world a little bit every day.

References

1. 2018 Economic Survey of India (Unwanted: 21 million girls report)

2. Growing up unequal study: HBSC 2016 study (2013/14 survey)

3. National Crime Record Bureau Report 2018

4. Rubin, Provenzano, & Luria, 1974 Research "The eye of the beholder: parents' view on sex of new borns"

5. Caldera, Huston, and O'Brien, 1998 Research "Social Interactions and Play Patterns of Parents and Toddlers with Feminine, Masculine and Neutral Toys"

6. Health citation: Wanic, R., Kulik, J. "Toward an Understanding of Gender Differences in the Impact of Marital Conflict on Health"

7. Full Article with Research Details: Daily Telegraph: "Married-men-are-happier-than-married-women"

8. Full Article with Research Details: BBC: "why-promoted-women-are-more-likely-to-divorce"

9. Full Article with Research Details: Witchwind: "Individualism-and-relational-deprivation"

10. PEW Research: Interatrial marriage trends amongst Asian Americans

11. Scott S. Hall, Rebecca A. Adams, Ball State University – "Cognitive Coping Strategies of Newlyweds Adjusting to Marriage"

12. Hall, S. S., & Adams, R. A. (2011). "Cognitive coping strategies of newlyweds adjusting to marriage. Marriage & Family Review, 47, 311-325

13. Laura K. Soulsby, Kate M. Bennett, Rodgers & White, 1993, Blumstein, 1975, Carter & McGoldrick, 1989 Research Titled: "When Two Become One: Exploring Identity in Marriage and Cohabitation"

14. Full article and research: "Over-nearly-80-years-harvard-study-has-been-showing-how-to-live-a-healthy-and-happy-life"

15. Full article and research: Indian Express " The impunity of Marital Rape"

16. Deniz Kandiyoti': Patriarchal Bargaining

17. Full Article and Research by Outlook: Glaring Orgasm Gap

18. Excerpt from Book by Moira Weigel: *Labour of Love: The Invention of Dating*

19. Full Article and Research by The Atlantic: How Long Can You Wait to Have a Baby?

20. Unintended Pregnancy and Abortion Worldwide Report 2022

21. Lancet Health Global medical journal 2019

22. Why the Halo Effect Affects How We Perceive Others (Simply Psychology, 2021)

23. Research by Subhashini Ganeshan, SL Ravishankar, Sudha Ramalingam: "Are body image issues affecting our adolescents? A cross-sectional study among college going adolescent girls (2018)"

24. Research by Inbal Gurari, John Hetts, Michael Strube: "Beauty in the "I" of the Beholder: Effects of Idealized Media Portrayals on Implicit Self-Image" (2010)

25. Research by Debra Trampe, Diederik Stapel, Frans W Siero: "The Self-Activation Effect of Advertisements: Ads Can Affect Whether and How Consumers Think About the Self"

26. Research by University of South Australia, Flinders University: "Impact of advertisement on mood"

27. Research by University of Nebraska at Omaha: "When Beauty is the Beast: The Effects of Beauty Propaganda on Female Consumers"

28. Body-Shaming + Cyberbullying report by national eating disorders organization

29. Break Binge Eating – A comprehensive list of statistical reports on body image

30. Periodic Labour Force Survey 2018

31. Excerpt from the book by Betty Friedman: The Feminine Mystique"

32. Workplace mental health Report (People Matters): "India's Mental Health Crisis"

33. Full Article and Research by Indian Express: Motherhood penalty in India

34. Full article and Research by Live Mint: Gender Pay Gap in India

35. McKinsey Research and Article: "Unconscious bias at the workplace"

36. McKinsey Research and Article: "Being the only one in the team"

37. Women and Leadership 2018 – Pew Research

Acknowledgement

To all the wonderful women I have had the privilege of meeting, knowing and understanding through my research. Your kindness, candour and solidarity changed my life.

Agrima	Gayatri. V	Mimi
Anna	Gunja	Mitali
Anshu	Ishita	Mona
Anuja	Joyeeta	Monica
Aparna	Juhi	Moumita
Apoorva	Jyoti	Nancy
Apurva	Kanchana	Neetu
Asmita	Kasturi	Nikita
Basanti	Laura. S	Nitya
Bhavana	Lucy	Noopur
Chandni	Mamta	Pallavi
Dipti	Manali	Pooja
Divya	Manishree	Pooja. C
Gayatri. D	Meenakshi	Pooja. M

Poulomi	Sakeena	Sonali
Pratima	Sangeeta. M	Sonu
Preeti	Sangeeta. P	Sujata. M
Priyanka. P	Sankhya Samhita	Sujata. S
Priyanka. R. B	Shamini	Tanvi
Rachna	Sharmila	Tapopriya
Rajashree	Shayantani	Urvarshi
Ripal	Shilpa	Vandita
Ritika	Shubhangi	Vidya
Rubina	Shubhonita	

My prayers for a petite figure or flawless hair might have been denied all my life, but that has been more than compensated by a bunch of lovely people who have always found their way into my life. Acknowledgement and gratitude are in order for many, and I share them below in no particular order:

> To my ma and baba for loving and supporting me even if I have missed their calls all through while writing this book.

> To my elder sister, Priyanka – the greatest guide, critic and friend. I have never been able to do anything worthwhile without her help.

> To my partner in life Aditya – the kindest human I know. You decorated my life!

My Sasu-Ma (Mummy) – your encouragement, discussions and questions have made me think more deeply and made this a better book.

To my friend, Poulomi, who helped kick start the research for the book many years back with her connections and suggestions. You always showed up when I most needed you.

To Sangeeta Mami – my go-to person for art suggestions, political *gyaan* and cheese dips.

To my friends, Manali, Juhi and Mimi, who have helped in growing the online community of Everyday Revolution. You guys are truly Feminist, Fierce, Fun.

To my friend, fellow-feminist and collaborator, Veena Hari, who shared her professional expertise as a psychiatrist and personal expertise as an amazing woman to inspire many parts of this book.

To my talented collaborator and cover designer Payal Sharma – thank you for your art and ideas. I am a lifelong cheerleader.

www.ingramcontent.com/pod-product-compliance
Lightning Source LLC
Chambersburg PA
CBHW032020150726
47990CB00005B/2045